Values,
Life-long Education
And An Aging Canadian Population

374
.971
V215

SEP 1 7 1984

Values, Life-long Education And An Aging Canadian Population

Douglas Ray, Ann Harley,
Michael Bayles and Others

Third Eye
London   Canada
1983

Canadian Cataloguing in Publication Data

Main entry under title:
Values, life-long education and an aging Canadian population

Selected papers from a seminar held at the University of Western Ontario, Oct. 1981.
Bibliography: p.
Includes index.
ISBN 0-919581-11-0

1. Continuing education - Canada - Congresses.
2. Adult education - Canada - Congresses. I. Ray, Douglas. II. Harley, Ann. III. Bayles, Michael D.

LC5209.V34 1983   374'.971   C84-098276-3

Photo Credits
Les Ste. Marie, P.91
Marina Quattroucchi, P. 92
UNESCO, P. 93

Published by
Third Eye Publications Inc.
Box 4640, Stn. "C", London, Canada
N5W 5L7

VALUES, LIFE-LONG EDUCATION AND AN AGING CANADIAN POPULATION

Price: $10.50

ISBN 0-919581-11-0

PREFACE

The Canadian population has been aging for many years. There are more persons now retired, there are relatively fewer children, the typical worker is more experienced. These changes can be studied for their present and future significance. It is possible to break down the overall projections to see what will be the numbers of young adults or older adults in society or in the work force; the numbers of men and women, the impact of international or domestic migration, of differential birth rates and the impact of health.

The interaction of such population studies with economic projections, public policy and especially educational needs and the best means of satisfying them is an academic and practiced exercise of great importance. Recognizing this, a research group of twenty two experts drawn from various parts of Canada, different vocations, both sexes and several age categories examined the topic in an interdisciplinary seminar at Spencer Hall, The University of Western Ontario in October 1981. Selected papers were subsequently revised for this publication.

ACKNOWLEDGMENTS

<u>Values, Life-Long Education and an Aging Canadian Population</u> was spurred by a statement by the late Roby Kidd that the values of pursuing different kinds of learning varied over the life time of every person. This idea was elaborated by the editors in consultation with several Canadians expert in the field: John Cairns, Jan Loubser, Gordon Selman, David Radcliffe, Betty McLeod, Paul Belanger, Jack Pierpoint, and Margrit Eichler. Papers that formed the basis of the chapters of this book were prepared and presented by their authors at an invitational seminar at Spencer Hall, The University of Western Ontario, in October 1981. Extended contributions were available at that seminar to help shape the arguments, particularly from Heather Lysons, Terry Morrison, Kamela Bhatia, David Balcon, and Arlene Hoffman. Reviewers of all or most of the manuscript included Jan Morgan, Paul Belanger, Deo Poonwassie and Guy Bourgeault.

The entire project was generously supported by the Social Science and Humanities Research Council of Canada with a "strategic" grant. The Department of Educational Policy Studies, Faculty of Education, The University of Western Ontario was responsible for manuscript preparation. Word processing was ably prepared by Susan Gmiterek, with additional typing by Dorothy Knight. Graphics were prepared by Liz Combes. Photographs were supplied by Les Ste. Marie, Marina Quattrocchi and courtesy of UNESCO. Les Ste. Marie provided production assistance. A special thanks is extended to David Radcliffe for his able contribution throughout, and to Jeanette Tran for her cheerful assistance.

The cover photo is of Hendrika Vlasman, recently retired from the Department of Educational Policy Studies, a person who exemplifies education as a life-long process. The photo was by Les Ste. Marie.

CONTENTS

Social Conditions

1. Introduction -- Values, Lifelong Education and An Aging Canadian Population 1
   Douglas Ray

2. Canadian Population Aging, with Projections 16
   Leroy Stone

3. The Relative Sizes of Selected Ethnic Groups: Forecasts of Natural Increase, Mobility and Cultural Choices 30
   Douglas Ray

4. Economic Projections for Canada with Some Implications for Employment and Education 40
   Betty Macleod

Educational Responses

5. Some Observations on Literacy in Canada and A Method to Improve the Match Between Reading Materials and Readers 94
   John Cairns and Kristian Kirkwood

6. Values of Canadian Adults and Technical and Vocational Education 117
   D. Stuart Conger and M. Catherine Casserly

7. Life-Long Education and Personal Fulfillment: An Exploration of Implications for the Later Years 137
   David Radcliffe

8. An Assessment of Existing and Emerging Third Age Continuing Education Programs for Social Awareness and Political Participation 147
   C.G. Gifford

v

CONTENTS

Educational Responses
continued

9. Personal Fulfillment Programs:
   A Practitioner's View 167
   Anne Ironside

10. Value Issues of Lifelong Education in
    an Aging Society 177
    Michael D. Bayles

11. Conclusions and Recommendations 195
    Douglas Ray and Janet Collins

    Bibliography 208

LIST OF FIGURES

Social Conditions

1.1 Percent Populations by Broad Age Groups, Canada, 1921-2001 4

1.2 Participation Rates by Age and Sex, 1966-1977 7

2.1 Percentage of the Population Aged 65 and 75 and Over, Canada, 1921 to 1981 and Projections to 2021 19

2.2 Ratio of Male to Female Population for Selected Age Groups, Canada, 1901 Through 1976 and Projections to 2021 21

2.3 Percentage of the Population Aged 65 and Over, Canada and Selected Countries, 1941 Through 1976 23

2.4 Life Expectancy at Age 0 and Age 65, Canada, 1961, 1966 and Projections for Five-Year Periods to 2016-21 24

2.5 Historical and Projected Total Fertility Rates, Canada 1921 to 1971 and Projections for Five-Year Periods to 2016-21 25

2.6 Age Pyramids by Sex Canada, 1960, 1980, and 2000 26

4.1 Job Vacancies (all categories) 45

4.2 Employment in Canada and Regions 47

4.3 Unemployment Rates by Region 49

4.4 Unemployment Rates for Canada by Sex and Ages 15-24, 25 and Over 51

4.5 Index of Personal Incomes Per Capita in Canada and Regions (Canada = 100) 55

LIST OF FIGURES
continued

Educational Responses

5.1 Population Within Age Groups Not Attending School Full-Time by Level of Schooling 101

5.2 Canadians Aged 15+, Not Attending School, With Less Than Grade 5 and 10 (Grade 9 in Newfoundland) ..102

6.1 The Values Selected for the International Study: Stage One 122

7.1 Personality Types and Aging 140

LIST OF TABLES

Social Conditions

1.1 Full-Time Post-Secondary Enrolment as a Proportion of the Relevant Age Groups by Level 9

2.1 Population of Canada by Selected Age Groups and Sex, 1901 Through 1976 and Projections to 2021 ...17

2.2 Projections for Key Age Categories: In the Total Population 18

2.3 Summary of Assumptions for Statistics Canada Projections 1 and 4, Canada, 1981 Through 2021 22

4.1 Indexes of Employment Growth by Sex, Ages 15-24 and 25 and over, for Canadian Regions (1975 = 100) 53

4.2 Annual Growth Rates in the Provincial Labour Forces and Their Components Over the Period 1971-1980 (per cent) 64

4.3 Employment Growth by Provinces (average annual per cent rates of growth) 65

4.4 Interprovincial Migration Flows (annual average '000) 67

4.5 Interprovincial Net Migration of Children and Adults (annual averages, '000) 68

4.6 Percentage Distribution of Population by Three Main Age Groups Medium Projection for Canada, Selected Years 75

4.7 Labour Force Participation by Sex, for Canadian Provinces in 1981 80

LIST OF TABLES
continued

Educational Responses

5.1 Illiteracy Among Canadians Aged 15+, 1961-1976 96

5.2 Canadian Population 15 Years and Over, Not Attending School Full-Time by Ethnic Group and Rank According to Highest Percentage with less than Grade 9, 1971 Census 98

5.3 Population Not Attending School Full-Time by Age Group, Showing Level of Schooling for Canada, 1976 Census 100

5.4 Population 15 Years and Over, Not Attending School Full-Time, Showing Level of Schooling for Canada and the Provinces, 1976 Census 104

5.5 Overall Literacy Rates by Grade and Subject Area for Ontario and Manitoba 111

CHAPTER 1

INTRODUCTION --
VALUES, LIFELONG EDUCATION AND AN AGING CANADIAN POPULATION

Douglas Ray

What are the probable future interrelationships among certain "facts" about society, several value emphases which may change periodically, and the educational `choices which they permit? The authors who address aspects of this general question accept education to be life long, with initial schooling merely laying the foundation for what follows. Different perspectives are likely to be associated with age: i.e., young adults emphasize career requirements, older adults seek to realize other yearnings. Women and men are also considered separately, not because their needs or interests always differ, but because many studies identify the human race exclusively with mankind. Overlap can be expected for both these classifications.

Our analysts accept as "facts" those choices affecting society where the decisions have already been taken (a child has been born and will live for many years) or where they are incredibly complex to control (different groups will experience relative growth or decline within the population; prosperity in Canada is affected by global conditions; new technology will undermine some jobs and create new ones).

Leroy Stone, Douglas Ray and Betty Macleod introduce these aspects of the study.

In the second section, several social choices which must be constantly reaffirmed are examined to learn their implications for life-long education. For example, there may be greater and more equal participation by women in the work force. "Productive" and "service" activities may be reevaluated -- even providing recognition for activities that are now labelled as "non-productive". We could adjust work hours, interrupt careers, revise career plans to meet new conditions, redefine the justification for retirement. We could ensure that certain kinds of education become more thorough, more "relevant", more status conferring, or more widespread.

Four arguments for life-long education for those who expect to be fully citizens of the future have been identified. Citizens must be able to understand and manipulate the symbols of our society. This means literacy at adequate levels, numeracy and linguistic fluency in dominant languages. Present knowledge of literacy, needed studies and educational consequences are addressed by John Cairns and Kris Kirkwood.

Citizens need financial security. Jobs call increasingly for more than willing and healthy bodies, they require technical and vocational skills. D. Stuart Conger and M. Catherine Casserly review some of the values of Canadian adults related to technical and vocational education.

Citizens must feel comfortable with their identity and lot in life, perhaps particularly as family, financial, and vocational patterns change rapidly in what Toffler called "Future Shock". This personal fulfillment role is explored by Anne Ironside and David Radcliffe.

Citizens must be able to understand and modify the relationships between themselves and society, especially that outside the workplace. It may involve finding, furthering or revising group affiliations or using available influence to improve social interactions. Awareness of the needs and hopes of others - even those who are far away - will combine with personal or ingroup interests in this kind of interaction and education. This part of the study will be addressed by Giff Gifford.

These complementary aspects of life-long education unite in a number of value questions. There may have to be choices among desirable situations, priorities set, sequences established. Identifying some of these values questions and lacing together the strands separated in the research to facilitate detailed analysis has been the task of Michael Bayles.

Aging Populations

An Aging Population means more than the biological process that signals advancing years by hardening arteries, failing eyesight, sagging muscles and a preoccupation with yesteryear. It also means more than the truism that every Canadian - even the tiniest baby - is aging; that we all enter life, strut our interval on stage, then leave our grieving relatives.

An aging Canadian population means the progressive shift in the distribution by age as the 1921 country of youth, which had 52% of its population under 25 and 5% over 65, evolved so by 1981 there were 41.7% under 25 and 9.7% over 65 (Figure 1.1). This aging will continue because of lower birth rate, increased life expectancy, and certain changes in migration patterns.

FIGURE 1.1   Percent Populations by Broad Age Groups, Canada, 1921-2001

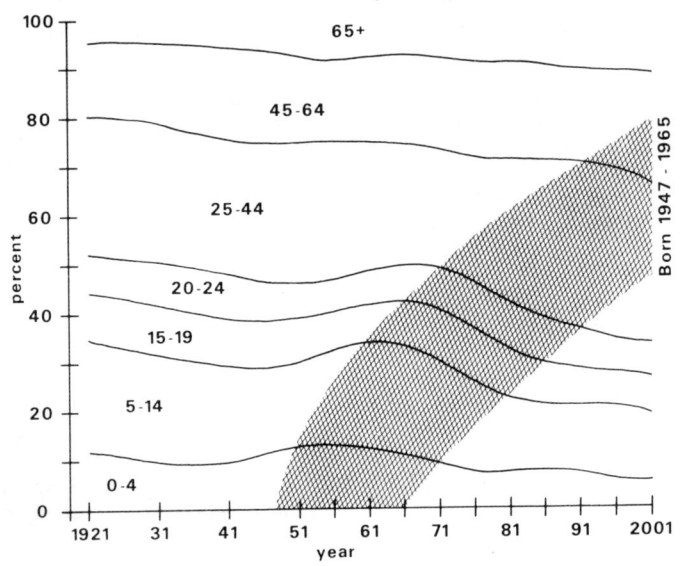

Sources: Statistics Canada, 1971 Census, Population Age Groups, Catalogue 92-715; Statistics Canada, Population Projections for Canada and the Provinces, 1972-2001, Catalogue 71-514, Projection C (fertility - 1.80, net migration - 60,000).

Life-long Education

The world changes. People forget. Together these two facts mean that schools can never provide knowledge and skills sufficient for a full life. Recognizing that, people continue to learn what they must throughout life, often in relatively simple and sometimes in exciting ways. The difference between learning and education is important. People learn or fail to learn according to their capacity to find appropriate information, master new skills, etc. Education involves the systematic provision of learning experiences in the attempt to make such knowledge and skills more accessible. More people can learn and can learn more effectively if good education is available (Cropley 1977).

Life-long learning and life-long education have been embraced by UNESCO as organizational principles since 1972, although they were advocated earlier (Faure 1972). In Canada the idea of life-long education is advocated by private and public, official and voluntary, national, provincial and local institutions. Overlap of function and competition for resources and clients is very general (Organization 1976). The market place chaos extends the other way too, for probably millions of Canadians have no ready access to the kinds of education they most need.

The Baby Boom

John Kettle has followed and predicted the progress through life of a particular group of people: the "baby boom", born 1952-1965. The substantial bulge of babies expanded rapidly, then after 15 years collapsed to its former level. The surge and decline disrupted the orderly plans of schools, youth facilities, universities and then the labour force. ·The impact on retirement, pensions and geriatric facilities is yet to come (Kettle 1980).

This study is concerned with the larger picture - the group before, the baby boom and its followers. In education the studies are quite complete. For example, the decline in birth rates from the high period of the "Baby Boom" resulted in smaller school enrolments affecting first elementary, then secondary and recently higher education. The declining numbers in the associated age groups have recently been masked by increased participation rates, i.e., by more persons voluntarily remaining in secondary schools or deciding to attend colleges or universities. Several important studies of the relationship between the size of the youth population and the requirements for teachers, schools, hamburgers, and books exist (Jackson 1978, Taylor 1980).

Schools and colleges are usually followed for both men and women by jobs, marriages, and babies. Recently the numbers of Canadians at this phase has declined: the decrease after the baby boom is already affecting the work force, markets, pay scales, productivity, etc. Voluntary decisions (to study, to work, to marry, to parent, etc.) make it more difficult to predict and plan for the economy and society than it was to provide schools. Women will make a huge difference in these plans: how many will enter and how long will each remain in the work force, what will be their aspirations for income and responsibility? There is still plenty of opportunity for expansion if that course is widely chosen (Figure 1.2). With a declining ratio of employed to dependents (including children and retired), what could be done to alter the assumptions about employability? What are the educational implications if a larger part of the women who are not presently seeking jobs are forced or induced to seek employment?

Figure 1.2 Participation Rates by Age and Sex, 1966 – 1977

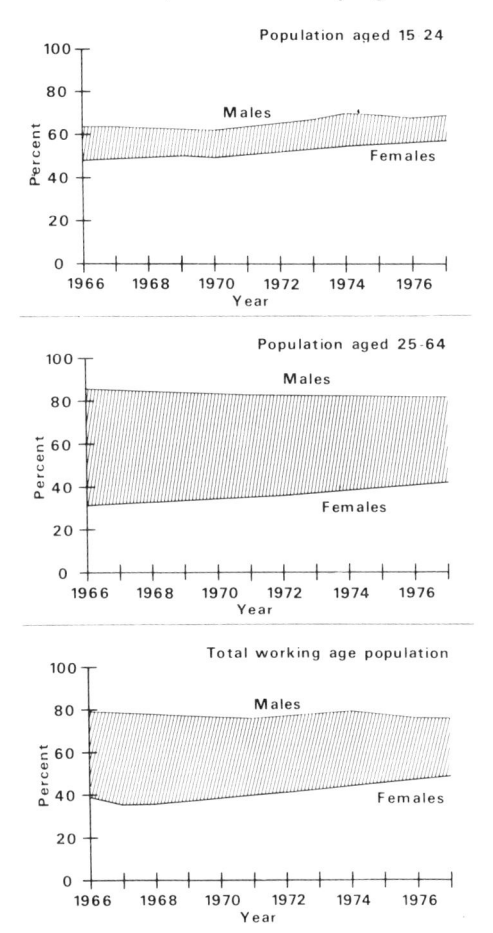

Population aged 15-24

Population aged 25-64

Total working age population

Source: <u>Historical Labour Force Statistics</u>, Catalogue 71-201, 1978.

Economic Decisions and Planning

The interaction between the economy, the work force and employment within Canada is very difficult to describe with precision. Who are included in our work force? and who contributes to our prosperity? These questions usually ignore or underestimate household contributions (mainly by women) and other activities outside the market system. Separate decisions within the private sector and by different levels of government (or in foreign countries) may be countervailing. The size of the dependent Canadian population (i.e., children, housekeepers, invalids, retired and those unable to find sufficient or suitable work) is significantly affected by managerial or bureaucratic decisions: profit margins, modernizing, interest rates, tax rates and political interests. So called 'dependents' continue to work at various tasks that may benefit society without being recognized in the Gross National Product.

The numbers in the work force can be adjusted fairly quickly by various means. Technological change or new resources drive people (especially women?) into or from the work force. They also affect the age of retirement. The economic health of a particular city, province, region, or the whole country affects both employment rates and migration. Particularly for those with able bodies and/or trained minds, there is a prospect of building careers and futures in another place - perhaps in a foreign country. Migration cannot be written out of the future of Canada.

Social Implications

There is an obligation of society to its dependent population, whether based on family love, humanitarian compassion or the contracts created as people defer part of their income (through taxes or other means) in the expectation of agreeable retirement conditions. The rapid growth of the ratio of retired to working Canadians is projected to continue (Economic 1979). For pensions, medical facilities and geriatric medicine, various types of retirement housing - and the financial problems associated with all of them - these changes are very significant (Lefebre 1979, Allentuck 1977, Auerback 1976).

"You are as old as you feel" according to an old song. Personal decisions to learn, marry, have children, work in a particular way, retire or move to a new location are only roughly determined by age. For example, participation rates at secondary and university levels continue to climb (Table 1.1) delaying entry into the work force. Retirement at 65 has experienced a steady increase since 1951 but those over 65 remain employable in many cases. Some of the 65+ (2,361,000 in 1981, growing to 3,387,300 in 2001) could be attracted again to the work force, particularly where the right working conditions exist or could be created. Part time employment is a possibility. Retirement at a particular age may neither be legally enforcable nor necessarily desirable (Senate 1979).

Table 1.1 Full-Time Post-Secondary Enrolment as a Proportion of the Relevant Age Groups By Level

Year	Non-university (as % of population aged 18-21)	University Undergraduate (as % of population aged 18-21)	Graduate (as % of population aged 22-24)	Total post-secondary (as % of population aged 18-24)
		per cent		
1951	3.2	7.0	0.6	6.0
1961	5.3	11.9	1.1	10.6
1966	5.9	15.6	2.4	14.2
1971	11.2	18.5	3.2	18.5
1976	12.6	18.6	3.3	19.8
1977	13.1	18.2	3.1	19.6

Source: Historical Compendium of Education Statistics, Catalogue 81-568, 1978: and Education in Canada. 1978. Catalogue 81-229.

For these reasons identifying particular ages or sexes
with an educational, occupational or citizenship role is
tenuous, based on convention rather than biological need.
Although this study distinguishes between young and old
adults, and men from women, the needs and educational
expectations within each of these sectors present many
variations. For example, we may distinguish the incomes and
participation rates in the labour force for men and women.
At present men predominate in the higher incomes and in the
labour force for those aged 45-65. In most of the families
involved, the wives do the housework and earn the lower or
secondary income. When the men in such families retire, the
amount and source of family income might change drastically
but the typical activities of the women remain little
changed. In effect the wife would cope with housework with
her husband underfoot unless the day was pleasant for golf.

Should retirement mean something quite different,
something that would enable husband and wife to do more
things together - baking bread, treading the boards or
whatever other activities they choose? In anticipation of
retirement, such questions probably have educational
implications for two persons instead of one.

Values

In the present discussion values are reflected in the
reasons given for social policies. Economic, political,
social, and moral reasons all depend on certain values. The
values may pertain either to individuals who participate in
an activity or the larger society to which they belong. The
values can be inherent in an activity (a job resulting from
new skills) (Baier 1973). Although the general values
considered here - personal fulfillment, productivity,
literacy, employment - are widely shared in society and
arguments for them are not controversial, the social policies
which best promote these values often are. Controversy may
stem from disagreement about the "facts", or from the
weighting of these and other values, for example when a
policy to promote one impinges upon another: as when large
"spending" on personal fulfillment education is thought to

detract from "investment" to increase economic productivity. Even the choice of words implies values. It is important to identify the options and trade-offs involved, to decide which policies are likely to achieve what they promise. Unsound arguments can be politically persuasive, but eventually society must pay the price in terms of disappointment and frustration. Nonetheless, it is still important to understand the values and policies they are claimed to support, whether or not the arguments for them are widely shared.

A few illustrations correspond with the principal classifications of education used in this study. They include both public and private arguments in each case. Literacy may be valued in itself or it may be viewed as a necessary but repugnant skill that must be mastered in order to achieve something of value. This possibility becomes more realistic when other techniques of communication are substituted for literacy (reading); numeracy at an advanced level (Faure 1972, 62-66) (calculus, statistics, etc.), skills in operating a computer, fluency in a language that has local or general significance at present (English, French, Japanese ...). Functional literacy refers both to the level of mastery and the ability to understand and to communicate with others in situations that are increasingly complicated.

Technical and vocational skills mean economic independence - at least if the field was well chosen. Those who persist in learning obsolete skills do so for other reasons - perhaps as a form of conspicuous consumption or to achieve other personal or political values (Dore 1976). Society has a special stake in ensuring that a great deal of education is justified by the economic argument because the educational costs cannot long exceed society's willingness to pay, and various forms of technical and vocational education (not necessarily schooling) are essential to productivity (Harbison 1973, Bacchus 1979). There are dangers in producing more skills of a particular kind than the markets are capable of absorbing, particularly if they are provided to a socially selected population (Foster 1965).

Personal fulfillment may at first be regarded as selfish
in a world calling for interdependence and sacrifice. This
may not be so when unemployment is about 10% of those
registered in the work force, when 25% of the adults aged
15-65 are not even registered in that force, when
underemployment (accepting a job that requires less than your
qualifications or working only part time) is very common, and
where 35% of the population are either in schools or retired.
Personal fulfillment for many of these persons is a means of
maintaining health, a positive outlook and avoiding the costs
to society of lassitude, crime and perhaps illness (Blaug
1974).

Political awareness and political participation are
values of particular consequence to democracies. They were
cited as reasons for introducing universal education by
Egerton Ryerson, David Goggin and others, with similar
arguments introduced in most parts of Canada. In life-long
education political values are most closely associated with
conscientization in the women's movement, grey panthers,
Indian organizations, etc. The objective may be personal, as
when a gay strives for acceptance and legal rights in a
straight society. The implication that political education
is liberating should be closely examined, for domestication
is equally possible and shifting from one set of myths to
another may not change the situation. There are both uses
and misuses of political education (Faure 1972, 57-60).

Finally, it may be observed that whatever values may be
imputed, education may not deliver the expected returns
(Skager 1978). The classic example is the person who learns
to value conservation, learns to make fishing gear and to
paddle noiselessly but still finds the "benefits" to be
expensive in time, effort and humiliation. Canned fish is a
lot like eating crow.

The social values of political awareness and political
participation reflect ideology. Traditional social values
are essentially conservative, but life experience may lead
people to realize their irritation with the values of many of
our dominant institutions. If formal education reflects only
traditional perspectives, it is likely to become irrelevant

to many of those who are students voluntarily. The state has no monopoly on education, particularly at this stage.

Two kinds of solutions are possible. It may be possible or desirable to diversify the value bases for life-long education by extending public funds to traditionally working class programs (like Frontier College) and/or to diversify the courses, faculty and programs of the public sector programs. Providing credentials that recognize and legitimize the social learning undertaken by organizations like trade unions is a possibility.

The second type of solution has been debated for years in social education, particularly for secondary schooling. It would seek values clarification rather than values imposition (Howe 1977). This approach would make for lively debates rather than implying that there are absolute answers, such as might be fostered by any of the value specific institutions (church, state, labour union, or vocational association).

REFERENCES

Allentuck, Andrew. *The Cost of Age*. Toronto: Fitzhenry & Whiteside, 1977.

Auerbach, Lewis & Andrea Gerber. *Implications of the Changing Age Structure of the Canadian Population*. Ottawa: Science Council of Canada, 1976.

Bacchus, M.K. "Structural Transformation as a Pre-Requisite for the Success of Non-Formal Education Programmes in Economically Less Developed Countries". *Canadian and International Education*, 8:2 (1979), pp. 83-91.

Baier, Kurt. "The Concept of Value" in Ervin Laszlo and James B. Wilbur (eds.), *Value Theory in Philosophy and Social Science*. New York: Gordon & Breach Science Publishers, 1973, pp. 1-11.

Blaug, Mark. *An Introduction to the Economics of Education*. Harmondsworth, Middlesex, England: Penguin, 1976, pp. 317-324.

Cropley, A.J. *Lifelong Education: A Psychological Analysis*. Toronto: Pergamon, 1977.

Dore, Ronald. *The Diploma Disease: Education, Qualification and Development*. London: George Allen and Unwin, 1976, Chapter 1.

Economic Council of Canada, *One in Three: Pensions for Canadians to 2030*. Hull: Canadian Government Publishing Center, 1979.

Faure, Edgar, et al., *Learning to Be: The World of Education Today and Tomorrow*. Paris: UNESCO, 1972.

Foster, Philip J. "The Vocational School Fallacy in Development Planning" in C. Arnold Anderson & Mary Jean Bowman (eds.), *Education and Economic Development*. Chicago: Aldine, 1965, pp. 142-166.

Harbison, Frederick H. *Human Resources as the Wealth of Nations.* Toronto: Oxford University Press, 1973.

Howe, Leland W. and Mary M. Howe. *Personalizing Education: Values Clarification and Beyond.* New York: Hart, 1975; and Martin Kaplan, "The Most Important Questions". *Oxford Review of Education,* 3/1, 1977, pp. 87-94.

Jackson, R.W.B. *Implications of Declining Enrolment for the Schools of Ontario: A Statement of Effects and Solutions.* Toronto: Commission on Declining Enrolments in Ontario (CODE), 1978.

Kettle, John. *The Big Generation.* Toronto: McClelland and Stewart, 1980.

Lefebre, L.A., Z. Zsigmond and M.S. Devereaux, *A Prognosis for Hospitals: The Effects of Population Change on the Need for Hospital Space, 1967-2030.* Ottawa: Statistics Canada, 1979.

Organization for Economic Cooperation and Development. *Report on National Policies for Education: Canada.* Paris: OECD, 1976.

Senate Committee on Retirement Age Policies, *Retirement Without Tears.* Ottawa: Canadian Government Publishing Centre, 1979, pp. 37-39.

Skager, R. *Lifelong Education and Evaluation Practice.* Hamburg: UNESCO Institute for Education, and Toronto: Pergamon, 1978.

Taylor, William. "Managing Contraction" in R. Farquhar & I. Housego (eds.), *Canadian and Comparative Educational Administration.* Vancouver: Department of Extension, University of British Columbia, 1980, pp. 160-176.

CHAPTER 2

CANADIAN POPULATION AGING, WITH PROJECTIONS

Leroy Stone

Growth of Population

The total population of Canada for both sexes is shown in Table 2.1, with actual population 1901-1981 and two projections to 2001. "Projection 1" is the high in a recent Statistics Canada projection and "Projection 4" is a reasonable low. (An even lower projection, which assumes zero international migration, has been done for experimental purposes.) This table reflects the projection that about the turn of the century we will have between 28 million and 30 million Canadians. By the year 2021, the projections show 30 to 36 million Canadians.

For ages below 65, the level of uncertainty in these projections becomes very substantial after the turn of the century, chiefly because of uncertainty about future levels of birth rate and migration. The uncertainty applies more to young populations; projections for those 65 and over are provided to 2021. Even up to 2031 we have a reasonably good fix on the population age 75 and over, unless we assume a Third World War or some new bacterial strain that kills us off with an unusually high rate.

- 17 -

Table 2.1   Population of Canada* by Selected Age Groups and Sex, 1901 Through 1976 and Projections to 2021
(In thousands)

*Includes Yukon and Northwest Territories

Year	Total Both Sexes	Total Males	Total Females	Age 55-59 Both Sexes	Age 55-59 Males	Age 55-59 Females	Age 60-64 Both Sexes	Age 60-64 Males	Age 60-64 Females	Age 65 and over Both Sexes	Age 65 and over Males	Age 65 and over Females	Age 75 and over Both Sexes	Age 75 and over Males	Age 75 and over Females
							Historical								
1901	5,371	2,752	2,620	162	83	79	142	76	69	271	139	132	88	45	32
1911	7,207	3,822	3,385	214	114	100	179	95	84	335	171	165	109	55	55
1921	8,788	4,530	4,258	281	149	133	240	127	111	420	215	205	130	63	67
1931	10,377	5,375	5,002	367	199	168	295	157	138	576	295	282	173	85	88
1941	11,507	5,901	5,606	507	275	232	407	219	189	768	391	377	241	117	126
1951	14,009	7,089	6,921	571	293	278	506	264	242	1,086	551	535	338	163	175
1956	16,081	8,152	7,929	629	322	307	525	266	259	1,244	622	622	409	197	212
1961	18,238	9,219	9,019	706	362	344	584	293	291	1,391	674	717	502	238	266
1966	20,015	10,054	9,961	816	413	403	663	330	333	1,540	717	823	581	263	318
1971	21,568	10,795	10,773	955	472	482	777	382	395	1,744	782	963	667	280	387
1976	22,993	11,450	11,543	1,019	492	527	905	436	470	2,002	875	1,127	748	296	452
1981	24,343	12,068	12,275	1,180	568	612	979	462	517	2,361	1,011	1,350	883	339	544
							Projection 1								
1986	26,331	13,053	13,278	1,183	577	606	1,116	519	597	2,626	1,094	1,532	1,018	381	637
1991	28,092	13,900	14,192	1,186	580	606	1,122	532	590	2,999	1,222	1,777	1,201	438	764
1996	29,642	14,647	14,996	1,243	606	638	1,125	534	590	3,275	1,319	1,956	1,355	478	877
2001	30,981	15,290	15,690	1,532	748	784	1,180	558	621	3,362	1,383	2,808	1,537	530	1,006
2006	32,258	15,906	16,352	1,907	926	981	1,451	689	762	3,624	1,440	2,183	1,646	565	1,081
2011	33,570	16,538	17,032	2,111	1,021	1,090	1,802	851	951	3,970	1,589	2,381	1,702	582	1,119
2016	34,871	17,159	17,712	2,352	1,153	1,199	1,995	938	1,057	4,558	1,842	2,717	1,759	602	1,157
2021	36,051	17,708	18,342	2,319	1,138	1,181	2,220	1,059	1,161	5,214	2,111	3,104	1,964	681	1,283
							Projection 4								
1986	25,440	12,607	12,833	1,172	573	599	1,105	515	590	2,601	1,084	1,516	1,012	381	637
1991	26,549	13,127	13,422	1,168	572	596	1,106	526	580	2,958	1,207	1,751	1,188	433	755
1996	27,412	13,528	13,884	1,215	592	623	1,102	526	577	3,218	1,299	1,919	1,334	471	863
2001	28,054	13,821	14,232	1,486	726	761	1,148	544	603	3,387	1,357	2,030	1,507	522	986
2006	28,565	14,053	14,512	1,831	888	943	1,402	666	736	3,527	1,406	2,121	1,609	544	1,054
2011	29,000	14,245	14,754	1,997	965	1,032	1,726	814	912	3,843	1,542	2,301	1,656	569	1,087
2016	29,323	14,377	14,946	2,211	1,086	1,124	1,882	886	997	4,383	1,773	2,610	1,703	585	1,117
2021	29,479	14,415	15,064	2,161	1,063	1,038	2,083	997	1,086	4,969	2,013	2,956	1,891	658	1,233

Sources: Dominion Bureau of Statistics, 1961 Census of Canada, Vol. VII.1, Table 2; Statistics Canada, 1971 Census of Canada, Vol. 1,2, Table 7; 1976 Census of Canada, Vol. II, Table II. Data for 1981 to 2001 are projections from Statistics Canada, Population Estimates and Projections Division.

The group aged 25 to 44 is of particular interest to this study. This group is speculated to grow from 7.1 million to between 8 and 9 million by 2011 (see Table 2.2). The group aged 45 to 64 will be increasing from 4.7 million today up to nearly 7 million at the turn of the century, and moving quite sharply up to about 8.5 million by 2011. The growth rate of these higher ages tends to increase through the second decade of the next century. One age group that is expected to show unusually fast growth, up to the second decade of the next century, will be that of the 75 and over category. This is expected to grow at well over 2.5% per year, which is unusually high within the national context.

The population in the peak ages of retirement (65 and over) is about 2.43 million now and is expected to be about 3-1/2 million at the turn of the century. This will be the result of an unusually rapid growth rate for the older population, and it will cause what is called the "aging of the population" (or an increase in the proportion of older persons in the total population).

Table 2.2 Projections for Key Age Categories: (thousands) in the total population

YEAR		0 - 24	25 - 44	45 - 64	65+
1981	(Actual)	10,140	7,184	4,658	2,361
	(Projected)	10,292	7,179	4,611	
1991	(H	10,562	9,312	5,219	2,999
	(L	9,511	8,956	5,124	2,958
2001	(H	11,369	9,218	6,931	3,462
	(L	9,341	8,656	6,669	3,387
2011	(H	11,741	9,039	8,821	3,970
	(L	8,870	7,957	8,331	3,843

Source: Statistics Canada, Population Projections Division.

Population Aging

In 1981 about 10% of all Canadians were aged 65 and over, and at the turn of the century approximately 12% of all Canadians are likely to be aged 65 and over. We are expecting a gradual increase in that percentage over that time period (see Figure 2.1). The aging of the population increases very sharply after the middle of the first decade of the next century when the Baby Boom Generation enters the peak ages of retirement.

Figure 2.1 Percentage of the Population Aged 65 and 75 and Over, Canada, 1921 to 1981 and Projections to 2021

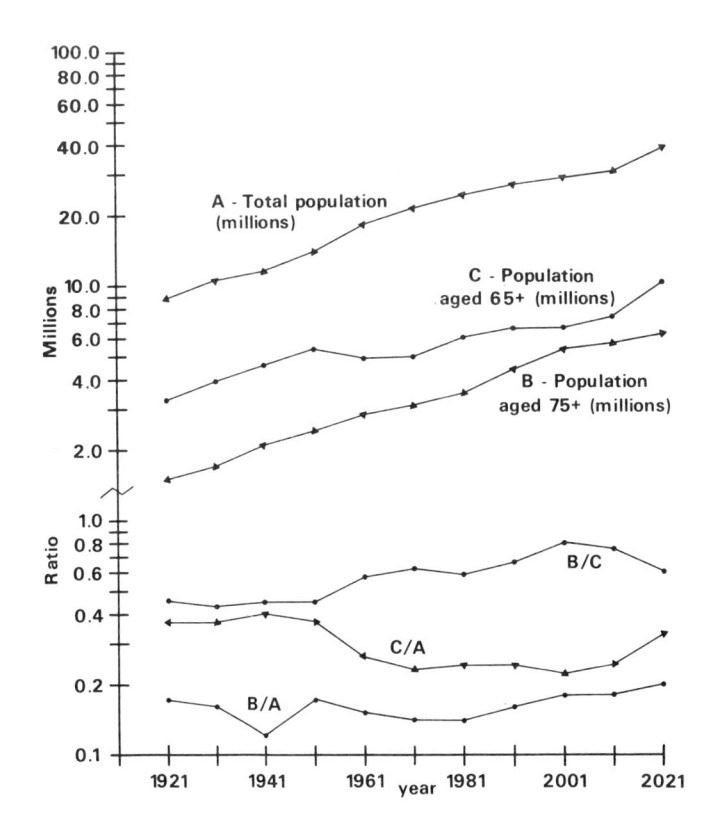

Source: Statistics Canada, *A Prognosis for Hospitals*, 1967-2031, Catalogue 83-520 E, p. 29.

The proportion of older persons in the population of Canada is much higher now than it was in 1900. This population aging has been very gradual, except during a period of about 20 years after the Second World War, when the birth rate increased substantially and the proportion of older persons in the population declined slightly. Gradual population aging began again in the 1960's (See page 4).

As population aging continues during most of the next 20 years, the number of persons who are at least 75 years old will grow *faster* than will the number of persons aged 65 to 74. Population aging will take place even *within* the older population! Also, during these next 20 years the ratio of men to women within the older population will decline substantially. This decline is already taking place in Canada, and it has been particularly steep since the early 1960's.

Figure 2.2 dramatizes that pattern. The vertical axis reflects the sex ratio, with 1.00 indicating that men were equal to women numerically in every age group. The horizontal axis shows the interval from 1901 to 2021. Since 1961 there has been a growing predominance of women. The ratio of women to men in the older population will climb quite substantially, until 2021, an effect most pronounced among those aged 75 and over.

Program Values

Adult developmental theorists characterize adulthood as alternating between periods of stability and change. Life/career planning programs and services are particularly useful for people in transition. In the recent study of the University of British Columbia's Women's Resources Centre, 82% of women described themselves as being in transition. The people who reported receiving the most benefit were those who described themselves as being in a state of readiness for change (Fournier 1981).

Toombs has observed (1978) that "For adults it appears that education may have less intrinsic value but more instrumental importance." Fifty-five percent of our clients are most concerned about their immediate job situation and educational choices which relate to their job.

Participants in women's programs report an increase in self-confidence, receiving acceptance, encouragement of self-directedness, control of life direction, information about opportunities available to them and consciousness of women's issues and an understanding of how this affects their lives.

One of our most provocative findings is that 73% of our clients reported an improved ability to develop and utilize social networks. Is life satisfaction directly related to this ability to develop and utilize social networks?

Life Planning/Learning Centres as Educational Brokers

Program provision is not enough: learning centres are a desirable link between learners and learning resources (Cross 1978). Though widespread in the United States, there are few of these educational brokerages in Canada. In Vancouver, the Centre plays an essential role, with eleven thousand drop-in and phone-in contacts in 1980. This centre is the "listening ear" of programmers to the emerging needs of clients.

A number of social commentators have spoken of the need

There is a widening gap in the mortality rates between older men and older women (Table 2.3), shown in life expectancy at ages 60, 65, and to a lesser extent, 80 and it has been widening for over 30 years now. It is a puzzling phenomenon that significantly affects several social problems with regard to family living, pensions, and the kinds of counselling and educational programs that are most needed.

Table 2.3 Summary of Assumptions for Statistics Canada Projections 1 and 4, Canada, 1981 Through 2021

Year	Projection I				Projection I			
	Fertility(1)	Mortality(2)		Net external migration(3)	Fertility(1)	Mortality(2)		Net external migration(3)
		Males	Females	(thousands)		Males	Females	(thousands)
1981	1.92	69.91	77.57	100	1.76	69.91	77.57	50
1986	1.99	70.22	78.26	100	1.73	70.22	78.26	50
1991	2.06	70.22	78.26	100	1.71	70.22	78.26	50
1996	2.06	70.22	78.26	100	1.71	70.22	78.26	50
2001	2.06	70.22	78.26	100	1.71	70.22	78.26	50
2006	2.06	70.22	78.26	100	1.71	70.22	78.26	50
2011	2.06	70.22	78.26	100	1.71	70.22	78.26	50
2016	2.06	70.22	78.26	100	1.71	70.22	78.26	50
2021	2.06	70.22	78.26	100	1.71	70.22	78.26	50

(1) Fertility (total fertility rate): number of children per woman that a cohort of females would bear if throughout their child-bearing period they had the age-specific fertility rates of the year in question and none of them died.

(2) Mortality (life expectancy at age 0): number of years an individual would expect to live if throughout his or her life he or she had the mortality rates of the year in question.

Net annual external migration: number of immigrants to Canada minus number of emigrants from Canada.

Source: Statistics Canada, Population Estimates and Projections Division, unpublished data.

Figure 2.3 provides an international comparison for a selection of countries with varying proportions of population age 65 and over. Several countries are far in advance of Canada so far as population aging is concerned; it is important to learn some lessons from them. In 1976 Canada was far below the level of Sweden. Even by 2001, the proportion of older persons in Canada will be less than it already is in Sweden. The Swedes are a good case to study because they have organized special education courses to which senior citizens are invited to participate. These are reasonably well attended and to a large extent are run by the aging persons themselves.

Figure 2.3   Percentage of the Population Aged 65 and Over, Canada and Selected Countries, 1941 Through 1976*

*Or nearest census year as appropriate

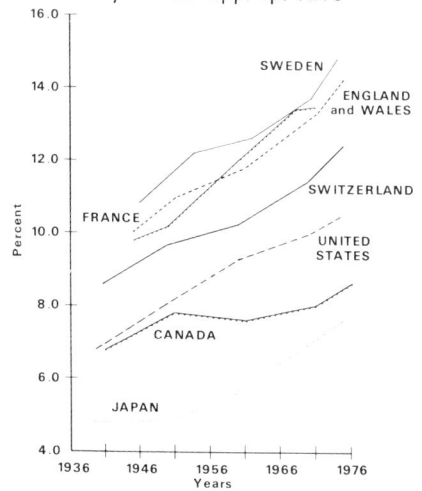

Sources: Statistics Canada, Perspective Canada II, Catalogue Number 11-508, 1977, Chart 3.31; 1976 Census of Canada, Vol. II, Table 11; United Nations, 1975 Demographic Yearbook, Table 7.

Assumptions

The assumptions that underly Statistics Canada's Projection 1 and Projection 4 (Table 2.1) are summarized in Figures 2.4 and 2.5. When these projections were made a decade ago, the 1981 total fertility rate was expected to lie between 1.8 and 1.9. It is now reported to be near 1.6.

Figure 2.4 Life Expectancy at Age 0 and Age 65, Canada, 1961, 1966 and Projections for Five-Year Periods to 2016-21

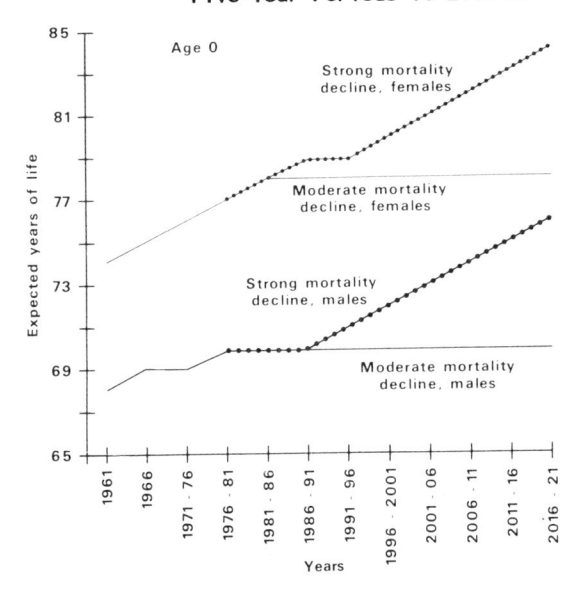

[Graph showing expected years of life from 65 to 85 on the y-axis, and years from 1961 to 2016-21 on the x-axis. Four curves are shown: Strong mortality decline, females; Moderate mortality decline, females; Strong mortality decline, males; Moderate mortality decline, males. The graph is labelled "Age 0".]

Source: Dominion Bureau of Statistics, <u>1961 Census of Canada</u>, Vol. VII.I, Table 2; Statistics Canada, <u>1971 Census of Canada</u>, Vol. 1.2, Table 7; <u>1976 Census of Canada</u>, Vol. II, Table II. Data for 1981 to 2001 are projections from Statistics Canada, Population Estimates and Projections Division.

Figure 2.5 Historical and Projected Total Fertility Rates, Canada 1921 to 1971 and Projections for Five-Year Periods to 2016-21

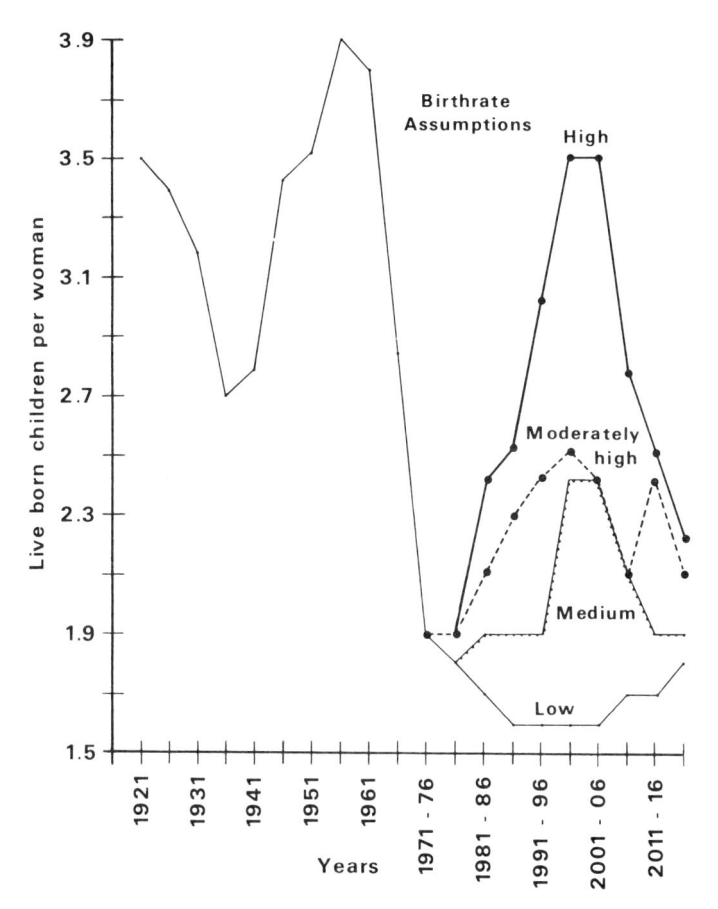

Sources: Statistics Canada, Vital Statistics Vol. 1, Births 1971, Catalogue Number 84-204, Table 10. Data for 1976 to 2021 are projection assumptions.

Figure 2.6   Age Pyramids by Sex

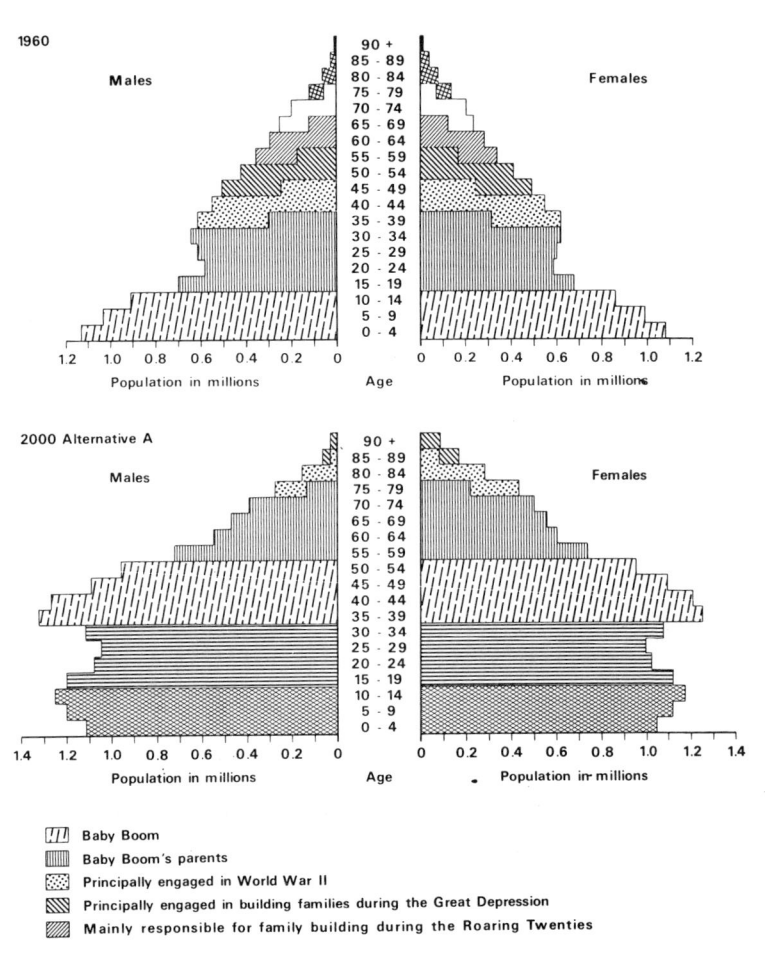

1960

(Age pyramid with age groups 0-4 through 90+, Males on left, Females on right, Population in millions from 0 to 1.2)

2000 Alternative A

(Age pyramid with age groups 0-4 through 90+, Males on left, Females on right, Population in millions from 0 to 1.4)

- Baby Boom
- Baby Boom's parents
- Principally engaged in World War II
- Principally engaged in building families during the Great Depression
- Mainly responsible for family building during the Roaring Twenties

Source: Statistics Canada,

Figure 2.6 cont'd.   Canada, 1960, 1980, and 2000

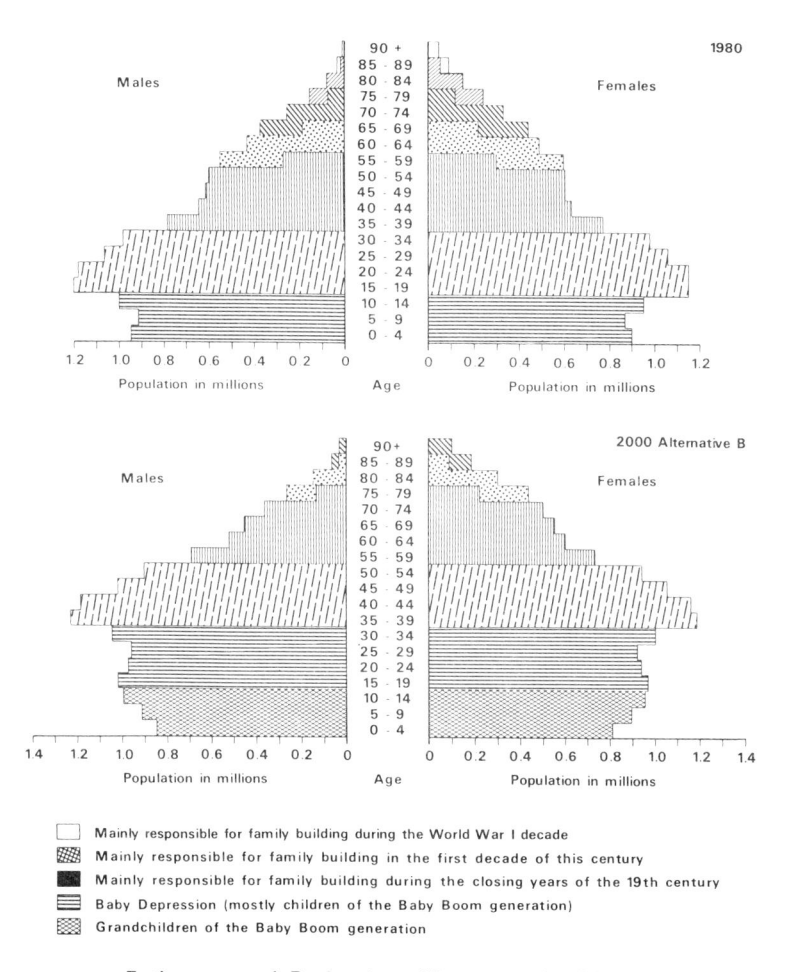

- Mainly responsible for family building during the World War I decade
- Mainly responsible for family building in the first decade of this century
- Mainly responsible for family building during the closing years of the 19th century
- Baby Depression (mostly children of the Baby Boom generation)
- Grandchildren of the Baby Boom generation

Estimates and Projections (Demography Division).

Summary

The flow of population from one age group to another over a period of time requires corrections for births, deaths and migration. The consequences of these forces to the year 2001 are summarized in Figure 2.6. It is important to note the relative and even absolute growth of the population aged 65 and over, particularly for women. These dramatic changes have profound implications for Canada's social policies. The most important of the educational implications are addressed by the authors of Chapters 5-11.

REFERENCES

Canada. Statistics Canada. Population 1921-1971, Revised Annual Estimates of Population, by Sex and Age Group, Canada and the Provinces. Catalogue 91-512. Ottawa: Information Canada, 1973.

Canada. Statistics Canada. Population, Revised Annual Estimates of Population, by Sex and Age for Canada and the Provinces, 1971-1976. Catalogue 91-518. Ottawa: Supply and Services Canada, 1979.

Canada. Statistics Canada. Population Projections for Canada and the Provinces, 1976-2001. Catalogue 91-520. Ottawa: Supply and Services Canada, 1979.

Marshall, Victor. Aging in Canada: Social Perspectives. Toronto: Fitzhenry and Whiteside, 1980.

Stone, Leroy O., and Susan Fletcher. A Profile of Canada's Older Population. Montreal: The Institute for Research on Public Policy, 1980.

Stone, Leroy O., and Susan Fletcher. Aspects of Population Aging in Canada, A Chartbook. Ottawa: National Advisory Council on Aging, Health and Welfare Canada, 1981.

CHAPTER 3
THE RELATIVE SIZES OF SELECTED ETHNIC GROUPS: FORECASTS OF NATURAL INCREASE, MOBILITY AND CULTURAL CHOICES

Douglas Ray

Comparative education has long included an academically dangerous tradition -- national character. It is dangerous because it dignifies and assigns a permanent character to social characteristics that are a response to particular situations, it masks differences within the group and it may posit glib and non-testable theory (Noah and Eckstein 1969). Despite these difficulties, it survives and is defended for certain applications. I propose to employ this controversial method for the present task, that of forecasting future populations for certain ethnic groups.

Canada is not a single society but a state that embraces many societies, different in their dimensions and objectives, constantly merging and regrouping as they evolve. The importance of this diversity for all public policy - including education - is generally acknowledged.

But it is very difficult to describe Canadian sub-societies in terms both precise and meaningful. The formal categories and relative precision of census data and immigration statistics do not provide clear implications for public policy. For example, there is a distinction between "religion" as reported by the census and evidence of conviction by several other measures. Identification of individuals with other census categories may be assumed to vary similarly. Language, ethnic origins, amount of formal education, evidence of wealth (telephones, type of bathroom) are all useful but not sufficient guides to the cultural values that matter to particular individuals, and the future cultural dimensions they would seek to promote - either as individuals or as a group (Kallen 1982).

Until recently we relied on undifferentiated population statistics for major social policies: how many school children, how many family allowances, how many old age pensions, etc. We have refined these for educational purposes, often assuming that education should reflect the largest language and religious divisions; and in the past making sex differences more important than now seem to be justified. Recently we have appended certain multicultural programs which were able to demonstrate community support. Many such divisions are most closely associated with primary education, but secondary and tertiary education also play their part in creating and maintaining group identity.

Social Distinctions Likely to Endure

Which social groupings are most likely to survive the various pressures to assimilate? The answers depend on which region of Canada we describe; for isolation from others, compact territory, proximity to leadership and distinctive social services are among the keys to survival. Migration may be an additional factor. If a group is periodically augmented by members from the same cultural group from outside Canada, its chances of retaining a distinctive identity may be enhanced.

Such questions become increasingly speculative if we project sizes and viability of cultural groups to secure policy guidelines for the future. Social policy including schooling will acknowledge then viable identities even though the details of loyalty may well differ substantially from our present preoccupations. As illustrations of the prospects of surviving assimilation processes, Canada in 2030 might be assumed to contain these distinctive groups, among others.

1. The Anglo-Celtic, not necessarily as a majority, but secure in their cultural identity. Regional differences may be quite important.

2. The French will also reflect regional differences, most important of which will be the Quebecois, for in Quebec the French are secure and confident to a degree unlikely in other provinces; the Acadians, particularly through the promise of bilingual status; and the Franco-Ontarians, if only because of their proximity to Quebec.

3. The Canadian Indians, but they will be neither homogeneous nor uniformly distinctive in their education and lifestyle, and the Inuit.

4. Isolated religious groups: especially Hutterites, Mennonites, Amish, and Doukhobors.

5. Ethnic/religious/linguistic minorities maintained by geographic cohesiveness, size and leadership - despite uncertain levels of immigration and a probable shift to heritage rather than mother tongue as a language justification: e.g., Ukrainians, Jews, Italians, and Germans.

6. Groups retaining a distinctive identity because of continuing migration and reinforced by distinctive race, language, religion, dress, etc., in various combinations, e.g., Chinese, Indians (Asian), and Caribbean populations.

The viability of various communities and their prospect for maintaining or securing culturally distinctive services (such as life-long education) are assumed to depend upon their size, leadership, cohesiveness and isolation. Within the overall population projections and economic futures of Canada, it is necessary to speculate concerning natural increase and migration. For selected examples from the groups identified, these factors are most likely to result in a relative increase; for some other groups, a relative decline is likely.

It might be added that many persons who appear to be associated with particular groups on the basis of paternal ancestry, religion, language spoken in the home, etc., may actually feel little allegiance to others of that group. They may be associated by choice and acceptance with other societies or they may have decided that such internal groupings have little significance for them. Although these feelings are often preludes to assimilation, that term implies that the drift of loyalties is always from the perifery to the center, neglecting the possibility of contests for loyalties (Kallen 1982). It is not apparent how language groups or ethnicity would be related to possible future interests like ensuring the survival of the family farm, nature preserves or particular handicrafts.

Forecasting the actual size and vigour of a cultural group departs from the precision of demographic data (as exemplified by Leroy Stone) and is strongly influenced but not determined by economic forces (like those discussed by Betty Macleod). It also reflects, for each Canadian, an individual response to ideals and social opportunities. One may aspire to and actually gain entry to social groups that had no value to one's parents. These individual realignments do not affect the total population figures but they may be important for social policy. Adjustments of government programs are likely to influence the results, perhaps usually in response to the trend of individual choices.

For each group we can calculate, after a selected interval or series of intervals like census years, its approximate size or fraction of the total group. The required data are the birth rate, death rate, immigration, emigration, adherence from other groups and dissidence (leaving for other groups).

$$CP = OP \left[(1 + (B - D)) (1 + (i - e)) (1 + (a - d))\right] \ldots (N)$$

where CP   is the calculated population, OP the original population.

B - D   the difference between birth and death rates, usually expressed as ratios per thousand.

i - e   the difference between immigration and emigration, also expressed as ratios per thousand.

a - d   the difference between adherents and dissidents, expressed as ratios per thousand.

N   is the number of intervals for which the calculations are repeated. If the differences hold constant, N becomes an exponent.

The whole formula expresses mathematically the consequences of those forces that we acknowledge but can never predict reliably. These forces include the decisions to have children, to seek to prolong life by any of several available means, to migrate in quest of jobs or sunshine or political freedom; to adhere to a social group for idealism, proximity; or to leave a group that cannot provide the critical mass needed for personal objectives.

Assumptions in Preparing These Forecasts

These forecasts are intended to reflect the probable population changes of particular groups, especially relative to that of the total Canadian projection. For example, the Inuit population may have a rate of natural increase four times that of the Canadian population as a whole because its birth rate may remain above the average while progress at extending life expectancy can be expected for some time. Although the relatively small Inuit population may well increase dramatically, it would still face the massive challenge to survival of its small size, wide dispersion and probable out migration and social dissidence.

The predictions are dispassionate to the extent possible. If the Dutch in Canada cease to consider their ethnicity to be a significant factor in their identity and choose to adhere to other groups, their disappearance as a distinctive group would be a fact but not a tragedy.

The numbers assigned, particularly to adherence and dissidence, would prove to be unrealistic if social policy including education created conditions dramatically altering the relative attractiveness of cultural integration or maintenance versus assimilation. Conditions outside Canada, either by creating or denying opportunity, will have profound impacts upon migration. These conditions cannot be reliably forecast.

Some Significant Groups Within the Canadian Population: Forecasts of Relative Change by 2031

French. A distinction can be made among the French in Quebec, those in Ontario and New Brunswick, and those in all other provinces. There is no reason to predict long term birth or death rates much different from the Canadian norm although recently the Quebec birth rates have been slightly lower than elsewhere. Immigration of francophones has been low, but Bill 101 of Quebec provides that migrants will be assimilated to the Quebecois community where possible. Domestic migration has traditionally been low and will likely remain behind that for other groups. The net changes will result in a small decline in the proportion of French in Canada but they will easily retain a majority in Quebec, they will remain significant minorities in northern New Brunswick and northeastern Ontario; but islands of francophones within the rest of Ontario, Western Canada and the Atlantic

Provinces beyond Acadia will be linguistically assimilated. Adherence and dissidence will be more important to French survival than birthrate or migration, and education will play its part (Rocher 1976).

Anglo Celtic. Although distinctions could be made among Canadians descended through remote AC lineage, those of remote AC background but an intermediate identification with the U.S.A., Australia, etc., and those recently migrated from the UK; these distinctions are rarely made. It is uncertain whether adherents from other ethno cultural groups (the Dutch or Swedes for example) should be distinguished either. The major point is that AC, the dominant group in all provinces but Quebec at present, is secure. Its natural increase will be near that of the nation as a whole. Its members may increase slightly from migration and are likely to increase substantially from cultural adherence and assimilation.

The Canadian Indians and Inuit seem likely to increase more rapidly than the average because of a high birth rate and a large potential for a reduction in the death rate (Indian Conditions 1980). Migration from and to the U.S.A. are assumed to balance one another. "Adherence" to Indian status may change dramatically as a result of formal changes in the Indian Act affecting persons of mixed Indian and white ancestry. The combination of these natural increases and more inclusive legal definitions may be offset in part by Indians who identify more closely with white cultures as a result of urbanization and diversified economic opportunities by 2031. Although numbers are difficult to assign, the "Indian" population by the probable new definition of the future, will probably exceed 1,000,000. They might be the third largest ethnic group in the country, passing the Germans, Italians, Ukrainians, Portuguese and Jews; especially since dissidence from these groups to the Anglo Celtic is likely to continue and Indian leadership may become more effective at maintaining adherence.

Hutterites are typical of the isolated religious groups. They can be expected to continue their population increase, although their traditionally high birth rates are beginning to decline. Migration to or from Canada is difficult to predict: adhesion and dissidence are assumed to remain low. In consequence, Hutterites will grow relative to the total but will remain only a small part of the Canadian population (Anderson and Driedger 1980).

Ukrainians appear to have birth and death rates very similar to those of the total Canadian population, and there is no reason to assume these will change. Immigration has recently been very low and this is expected to continue. Adherence is assumed to balance dissidence, both at very low levels. The Ukrainians and Baltic nationals, unlike most other ethnic Canadians, have lost their homeland as a cultural reservoir and as a result may remain unusually conscious of their identity within Canada (Lupul 1974). However, without periodic fresh infusions there would be a decline for this group's share of the Canadian population.

Italians and Portuguese appear to have a small natural increase, at least partly because migration has been fairly recent so the groups are a young population (see Leroy Stone). Immigration cannot be reliably predicted but it is assumed to exceed emigration. Although adherence and dissidence are both currently low they are assumed to rise at roughly equal rates. Consequently, depending upon natural increase and migration, the population of Italian and Portuguese Canadians is likely to grow faster than the population as a whole.

Racially Identifiable Migrants. Each of the racially identifiable groups present a different situation. The most difficult question is the impact on migration of conditions in Canada and elsewhere and their refection in Canadian immigration policy. It is assumed that Chinese families in Canada will have birth rates and lifespans typical for Canada, but the Chinese of Canada is still a young population. Immigration is predicted to remain above emigration, with the differences a major contribution to population increase. Adherents are expected to be low, dissidence only slightly higher. The net effect would be growth at significantly above the national average.

Caribbean populations are expected to grow rapidly at

first from natural increase and migration of relatively young families. Many years later the population will age. Adherence is assumed to balance dissidence.

One may conclude that Canada will continue to be dominated by the two "founding nations," with the native Canadians returning to major importance, with those of European descent gradually losing their distinctive cultural loyalties and with Asians and Caribbean populations becoming important minorities. This would merely accept for the future the trends established over a century of cultural diversification (Anderson and Frideres 1981).

The implications of these slight shifts among the population may be of greatest consequence to the areas of communication and social interaction, but even technical and vocational education may be affected. The ability of Canadians from various ethnic origins to integrate for a variety of activities has always been demonstrated but the psychological need for a feeling of cultural identity or even distinctiveness must also be recognized. This seems to imply that life-long educational programs must be devised to respect diversity, perhaps by responding to initiatives by various cultural communities rather than by imposing existing political divisions. The political implications of such a realignment of responsibility might reduce the significance of provincialism (Ray 1978).

REFERENCES

Anderson, A.B. and L. Driedger. "The Mennonite Family: Culture and Kin in Rural Saskatchewan", in K. Ishwaren (ed.), *Canadian Families: Ethnic Variations* (Toronto: McGraw-Hill, 1980).

Anderson, Alan B. and James S. Frideres. *Ethnicity in Canada: Theoretical Perspectives* (Toronto: Butterworth, 1981).

Indian Conditions (Ottawa: Indian Affairs and Northern Development, 1980).

Kallen, Evelyn. *Ethnicity and Human Rights in Canada* (Toronto: Gage, 1982).

Lupul, Manoly R. "Some Implications of Bilingualism and Multiculturalism for Curriculum Development," *TEMA* 6:12:17 (Dec. 1974).

Noah, Harold J. and Max A. Eckstein. *Toward a Science of Comparative Education* (Toronto: Collier Macmillan, 1969).

Ray, Douglas. "Cultural Pluralism and the Reorientation of Educational Policy in Canada", *Comparative Education* 14:1 (March 1978), 19-32.

Rocher, Guy. "Multiculturalism: The Doubts of a Francophone" in *Multiculturalism As State Policy* (Ottawa: Canadian Consultative Council on Multiculturalism, 1976), 47-53.

CHAPTER 4

ECONOMIC PROJECTIONS FOR CANADA WITH SOME IMPLICATIONS FOR EMPLOYMENT AND EDUCATION

Betty Macleod

Introduction

Economists have become increasingly reliant upon the development of macroeconomic models of the economy -- and particularly econometric models -- for the anticipation of economic futures. Such models depend upon numerous assumptions about population growth; the rate of discovery and exploitation of natural resources; the pace of industrial and technological development; the propensity of individuals, businesses and government to consume, save, and invest; the work participation, skills and productivity of the labour force; the rate of inflation and its effect upon real growth and gross national product; the significance of foreign markets and finance; the pattern of external trade; and other data. The list could be extended. A model should incorporate indicators for all the important functions in the economy and reflect the dynamic interactions of those indicators through a basic system of equations. Changes in the economy require revisions of the indicators or equations, or both. Such changes may drastically alter results, not only directly but also indirectly, due to the interdependence of many of the elements of the economic system.

Recent Experience with Projected Economic Conditions

Projections for Canada's economic future vary from piece-meal discussions by public relations directors of trade unions through speeches by finance ministers, reports by the Science Council, by the Conference Board of Canada, studies by the Institute for Research on Public Policy, by the Howe, Hudson and Fraser Institutes, and reports by international agencies such as the International Monetary Fund (IMF) and the Organization for Economic Co-operation and Development (OECD) which assess the economic progress of Canada along with other countries. The work of the Economic Council of Canada (ECC) is by far the most prodigious and intensive operation in the field. The economic projections used here are from the ECC's Nineteenth Annual Review, Lean Times, published in the fall of 1982.

The ECC viewed the most important influences on the economy over the next five years to be those associated with the external environment, energy (including supply, demand and price), fiscal and monetary policy, the rate of personal savings and the level of wage expectations. It established a set of working assumptions for a base projection, then adjusted these assumptions to obtain the most favourable and the least favourable outcomes. Alternative federal policies which might improve the economy were also discussed.

For 1982-87, Lean Times projected for the Canadian economy:

-- Real Growth: after a decline of 2.4% in 1982, real growth measured by gross national expenditure, will increase on an average of 2.8% over the next five years. This will be below potential levels throughout the period.

-- Inflation: expected to decline from 11.4% in 1982 to below 8%, trending downward to just over 7%. Inflation in Canada is likely to remain higher than in the US.

-- Unemployment: this will remain above desired levels, even though employment prospects will keep pace with labour force growth towards the end of the period. Little improvement is expected in unemployment which may average about 10% for the projection period.

-- Labour Productivity: will increase at a rate just below 1% per annum for the early years with possibly some improvement from 1985. Levels will remain below past and potential performance.

-- Wages: real wages will rise slightly, whereas nominal wages for 1983 and 1984 will be contained by the federal government's 6 and 5% ruling. If this program extends to other sectors of the economy, the real wage will fall in 1983 and 1984, with some improvement in succeeding years.

-- Personal Savings: changes in personal savings have been a major factor in both containing inflation and in retarding business profits and employment levels. In 1982 personal savings were about 13.1%, compared to 10% over 1976-80. The rate of savings appeared to have risen both as a buffer against inflation and as a consequence of higher levels of real interest (i.e., the difference between the nominal interest rate and the rate of inflation).

-- Government Receipts and Expenditures: have been contained by a lower level of oil prices than anticipated and the undermining of the income structure by unemployment. Both had the effect of reducing government receipts, while unemployment also increased government expenditures through unemployment insurance and welfare programs. Debt servicing charges, associated with the high federal deficit, will continue to exert upward pressure on government debt.

-- Current Account Balance of International Payments: may improve slightly due to Canada's energy resources and the low value of the Canadian in relation to the US dollar. However, much will depend upon US rates of growth over future years since Canada's economy has become increasingly dependent upon the US. The expected US rate of growth from 1983 to 1987 is about 3%. The policies for financing federal deficits in both the US and Canada will be significant determinants of the balance of payments. The US handling of the inflation problem is also important in a negative sense: if the US reduces inflation while Canada's inflation remains higher, Canada will be less able to compete with the US on world markets.

In its 1981 review, Room to Manoeuvre, the Council had indicated that the main thing going for Canadian prosperity in the immediate future was high domestic energy investment. This influence was expected to continue into the more distant future with several major energy projects ongoing over the decade, and indeed until the year 2000. A year before, in A Climate of Uncertainty, the ECC had concluded "that increased domestic supply and substitution of alternative domestic energy sources for imports would bring considerable long-run improvement in Canada's balance of payments. But cancellation of many of these large projects would lead to lower growth in the early part of the decade and to a worsening trade deficit at the end of the decade" (ECC 1980, p. 45). As projected, delay and cancellation of some megaprojects has had a dampening effect on expected levels of economic activity.

Medium to long term projections have not been particularly successful recently because of rapid shifts among the economic circumstances and policies of some major international traders. Canada is unusually vulnerable. For the future there is optimism in agriculture, energy, high technology, steel, and a few manufactured products where our industry is quite competitive (STOL aircraft, subway equipment, for instance). Many other areas reveal declining markets and a loss by Canadian industry of competitive advantages: e.g., mining, forest products, fishing, automotive manufacturing, furniture, textiles, shoes. These huge industries all now require modernizing programs with significant implications for employment.

In the view of the ECC, there is important structural weakness in the economy which is inhibiting Canada's growth. Transportation and distribution facilities are on too small a scale; the organization of fishing and agriculture needs updating; high unemployment persists in spite of skill shortages in some lines of production; and technology, production mix, and education and training programs have not been adjusting effectively to the emerging needs of the '80s (Lean Times 1982, p. xii).

Distribution of Prosperity by Region

Traditionally, differences in prosperity across the regions have been explained in relation to the distribution of natural resources, differences in transportation costs, and the size of the base population of an area. Some studies, particularly Natural Resources and Regional Disparities (Copithorne 1979) have included technology, economics of scale, labour quality, aggregate demand, and urban structure.

In earlier centuries, and to some extent until World War II, natural resources and transportation controlled where, and to what extent, growth would occur in Canada. The staple industries like fishing, furs, lumber, and wheat were unevenly distributed, favouring the development of regions, each stimulating a network of complementary goods and services. As production expanded and diversified, and as government policies made their impact, the benefits from these activities have become more evenly spread; but differences persist in employment, level of income, and social and cultural amenities.

Figure 4.1 indicates the pattern and number of job vacancies across Canada over the years 1971 through 1978. The data used for this figure refer to full-time, casual, part-time, seasonal or temporary work in all industries except agriculture, fishing, trapping, domestic service and non-civilian components of public administration and defence (Canada, Statistics Canada 1979, Table 4). The pattern shows Ontario at the top over the years 1971-78, followed by the Prairies and Quebec, with the Pacific and Atlantic regions having the fewest openings. Around 1974 the Prairie region began to outstrip Quebec.

Figure 4.1   Job Vacancies (all categories)

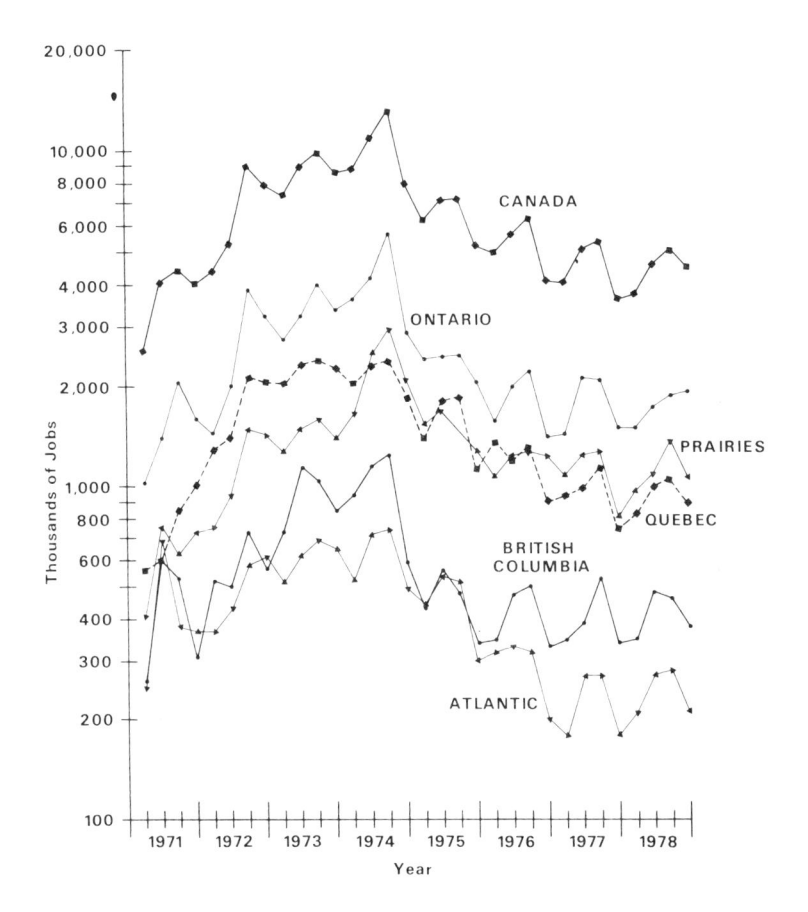

Source: Statistics Canada, Annual Report on Job Vacancies, Catalogue 71-203 Annual (to 1978) Table 4. Data above include full-time, casual, seasonal and part-time jobs.

British Columbia and the Atlantic region alternated respecting the lowest numbers of vacancies in some years, but British Columbia was generally higher. The quarterly vacancy survey upon which these data are based has been discontinued, so that we are unable to review changes since 1978. A help-wanted index for Canada and regions, available from 1962, uses the 1969 data as the base for each region, so that one may not easily compare changes across regions.

Figure 4.2 shows the growth of employment in Canada and regions since 1966. Steady growth in numbers employed occurred over all regions of Canada to 1981, but employment declined generally in 1982. The recent fall-off in employment was greatest in Quebec and British Columbia (-5.4% and -5.1% respectively). Employment in the Atlantic region fell by almost 3% between 1981 and 1982. Next came Ontario with a decline of 2.6%, and finally, the Prairies, where employment fell 0.9% between the two years. Although employment declined in both the Atlantic and Prairie regions, most of the jobs lost were in the provinces of New Brunswick and Alberta. Employment across Canada declined by 3.3% between 1981 and 1982.

Figure 4.2 Employment in Canada and Regions

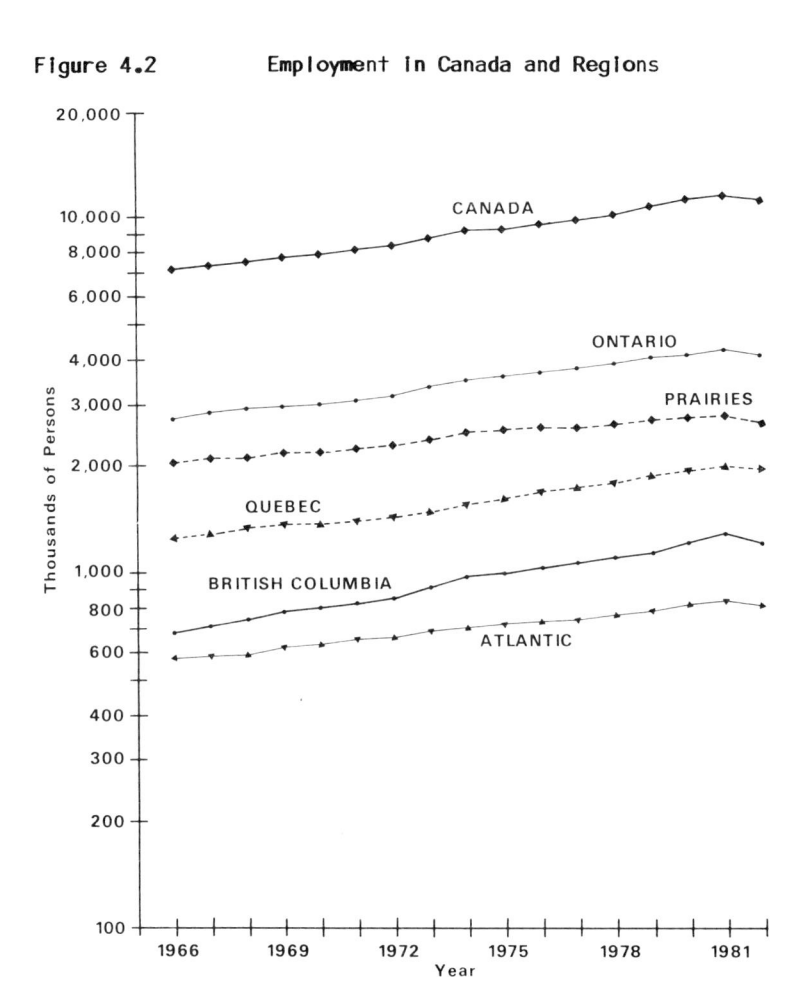

Source: Department of Finance, Economic Review, April 1982, for years 1966-81, Reference Table 31, p. 157; Statistics Canada, Canadian Statistical Review, January 1983, Table 5, p. 44 for 1982.

More familiar is the rate of unemployment, which is shown for Canadian regions in Figure 4.3. The highest levels of unemployment are where there was the least growth in employment prior to the 1982 turn-around, that is, Quebec and the Atlantic region -- especially in Newfoundland with 16.9% unemployment in 1982. The Prairie region had a relatively high rate of employment growth and the lowest rate of unemployment before 1982. Ontario and British Columbia do not quite fit the expected pattern. Rates of employment growth and rates of unemployment were both rather high in British Columbia before the 1982 decline, and by 1982 unemployment was 12.1%. In Ontario, which had the highest rate of employment growth of any region in earlier years, unemployment was 9.81% in 1982, higher than in the Prairies but lower than in other parts of Canada.

Figure 4.3 Unemployment Rates by Region

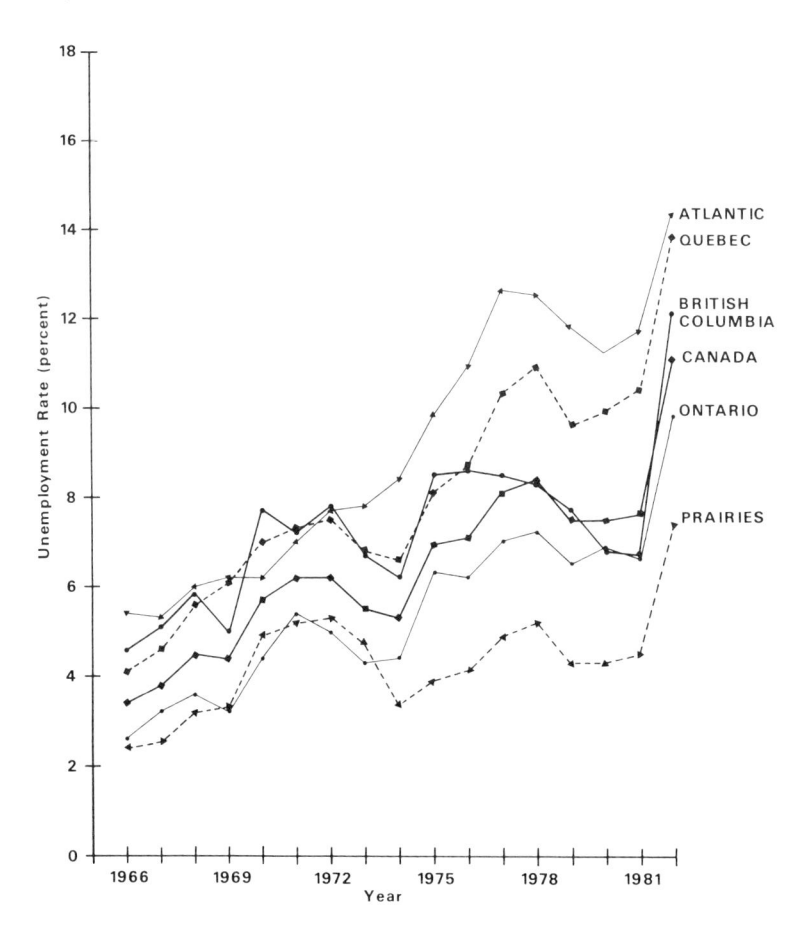

Sources: Department of Finance, Economic Review, April 1982, for years 1966-81, Reference Table 33, p. 159; Statistics Canada, Canadian Statistical Review, January 1983, Table 5, p. 47 for 1982.

Among the more interesting features of recent rates of unemployment are the differences for men and women, and for young people as compared to older workers. Trends are shown for Canada in Figure 4.4. Clearly the incidence of unemployment is much higher for workers under 25 years of age, and is highest for young men. Women 25 and older, on the other hand, have higher rates of unemployment than do men of those ages. However, these data may be somewhat misleading. The rates express unemployment in relation to the number of persons who are actively seeking jobs, and if any group is more easily discouraged than others so that the members "drop out", the rate will be artificially low. If discouragement is different for men and women, or for persons in different age groups, the rates for unemployment will be lower for the group with highest drop-out tendencies. This is a possible explanation of unemployment rates which are lower for young women than for young men.

Figure 4.4   Unemployment Rates for Canada by Sex and Ages 15-24, 25 and Over

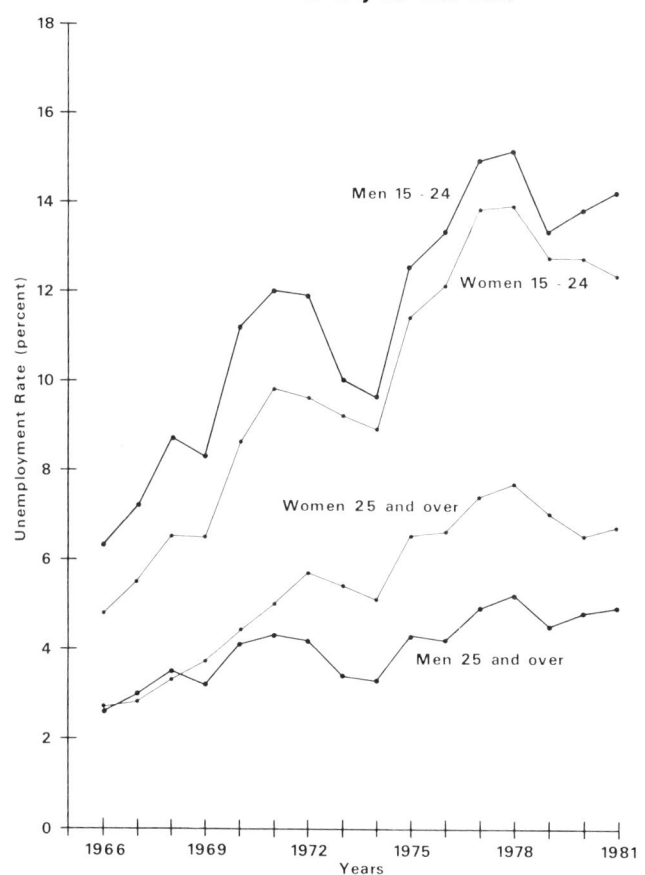

Source: Statistics Canada, Labour Force Survey Group, <u>Historical Labour Force Statistics</u> 1981 Ottawa: Statistics Canada, Cat. 71-201, pp. 163, 165, 168, 170.

To what extent does regional variation account for the differentials in employment by sex and by age (15-24 and 25 years and older)? Regional unemployment rates by sex and age are not available, but employment rates by sex and age may yield some clues. Table 4.1 presents indexes of employment growth in the regions for men and for women aged 15-24, and aged 25 or more, over the years since 1975 when these data first became available. For Canada as a whole the employment growth since 1975 has been about the same for younger and older men, while women -- particularly women aged 25 or older -- have benefited more than either male age group. The growth in employment of women in the older age group was over 30% across all regions, even in Quebec, where employment growth was generally lowest. Employment of older males grew faster in the Atlantic and Prairie regions and in British Columbia than elsewhere and was slowest in Ontario and Quebec, particularly Quebec with only a 4% increase over the period. Younger males were least favoured in the Atlantic and Quebec regions and made the largest employment gains relative to older men in Ontario and British Columbia.

Table 4.1 Indexes of Employment Growth by Sex, Ages 15-24
and 25 and over, for Canadian Regions
(1975 = 100)

Year	Canada Male	Canada Female	Atlantic Male	Atlantic Female	Quebec Male	Quebec Female	Ontario Male	Ontario Female	Prairies Male	Prairies Female	Br. Columbia Male	Br. Columbia Female
Ages 15-24												
1975	100.0	100.0	100.0	100.0	100.0	100.0	100.0	100.0	100.0	100.0	100.0	100.0
1976	100.0	101.5	98.2	100.0	97.1	99.3	99.6	102.2	105.2	107.0	102.3	95.7
1977	101.4	102.1	99.5	105.8	97.1	96.6	102.8	103.5	106.0	110.7	105.3	97.4
1978	104.1	105.9	100.0	108.1	95.9	99.6	107.5	113.3	109.2	113.4	106.8	102.2
1979	109.7	111.8	105.4	107.0	102.9	102.8	114.0	115.7	111.6	121.5	112.0	109.4
1980	110.7	114.9	106.3	112.8	102.3	103.1	114.0	117.2	115.0	127.4	111.8	115.4
1981	110.5	115.8	101.8	113.9	99.4	102.1	118.4	118.4	116.0	128.0	122.0	120.5

Year	Canada Male	Canada Female	Atlantic Male	Atlantic Female	Quebec Male	Quebec Female	Ontario Male	Ontario Female	Prairies Male	Prairies Female	Br. Columbia Male	Br. Columbia Female
Ages 25 and over												
1975	100.0	100.0	100.0	100.0	100.0	100.0	100.0	100.0	100.0	100.0	100.0	100.0
1976	101.3	105.1	101.7	103.8	100.1	105.9	101.6	103.5	102.0	108.0	102.6	105.6
1977	102.3	109.2	102.0	108.1	99.8	110.6	102.4	107.3	104.7	113.0	105.3	108.7
1978	104.1	116.4	106.3	117.5	100.5	117.1	104.4	113.3	107.6	121.0	105.5	119.8
1979	106.8	122.3	108.5	121.6	103.0	121.6	106.3	120.5	111.6	128.4	110.3	122.2
1980	108.4	129.7	110.5	132.5	103.8	130.2	106.6	125.7	115.0	137.2	115.4	130.5
1981	110.0	137.3	111.7	138.8	104.0	135.2	109.2	132.3	118.7	147.9	118.0	144.0

Source: Based on data in Statistics Canada, Historical Labour Force Statistics 1981, Cat. 71-201 Annual. Ottawa: Statistics Canada.

As we might expect, the differences in patterns of employment growth and in rates of unemployment affect patterns of income distribution across Canada. Figure 4.5 shows the variations in personal incomes in Canadian regions over the period 1950-1980. Although trends are not shown for earlier years, the ranking of regions by level of income has not differed much since the 1920's. British Columbia and Ontario have maintained the highest per capita incomes in Canada over the years, while the Atlantic region and Quebec have been lowest. Income in the Prairie region, above average in 1926, fell to around 70% of the Canada average in the 1930's, and fluctuated upwards after 1940; in some recent years Prairie income has exceeded the average for Canada. Alberta has now overtaken Ontario and is vying with British Columbia for top position. In current dollars, Alberta and British Columbia both had an average income of over $11,000 in 1980, compared with $10,600 in Ontario, the Yukon and Northwest Territories; $9,000 in Quebec and Saskatchewan; $7,000 to $8,000 in Manitoba, Nova Scotia, New Brunswick and Prince Edward Island; and $6,300 in Newfoundland (Canada, Department of Finance, 1982, Reference Table 17, p. 140). The rate of growth of real personal income per capita, expressed in 1971 dollars, was 7% over the period 1971-74, then fell to 2.7% for 1974-79, and was only 0.4% in 1980 (Ibid., Tables 17 and 43, p. 140 and p. 169 from which estimates were calculated).

Figure 4.5 Index of Personal Incomes Per Capita in Canada and Regions
(Canada = 100)

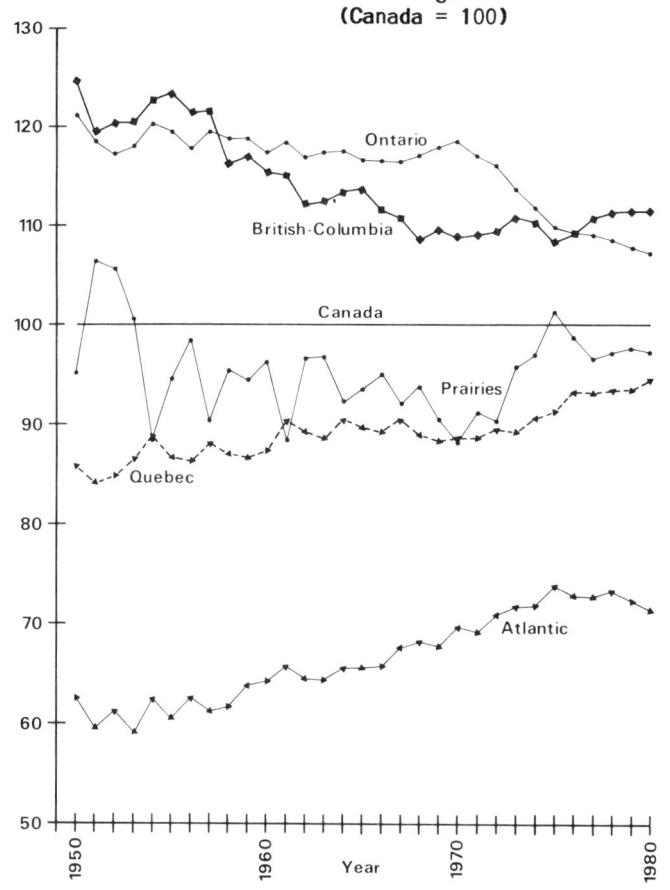

Source: Based on data in Department of Finance, Economic Review, April, 1980, Reference Table 19, pp. 175-176, and April, 1982, Reference Table 17, pp. 140-141.

In general, regions with the fastest rates of employment growth and the lowest rates of unemployment are also the regions with highest per capita income. These in turn are associated with greater availability of many social and cultural amenities. Ontario, British Columbia, and, more recently, Alberta, with top rates of employment growth and highest levels of per capita income, had the least crowded housing, most telephones per 100 inhabitants, most free-practice physicians, highest percentages of population aged 16 attending elementary and secondary schools (in 1974-75), and highest average salaries of university teachers (in 1972-73) (ECC 1977, p. 58, Table 4-11).

Types of Available Employment

Changes in employment opportunities across the regions are studied in <u>Regional Aspects of the Evolution of Canadian Employment</u> prepared for the ECC (Martin 1976). The study analyzes employment trends in Canada over the period 1961-70, comparing regional variations with either the rate of growth of the Canadian economy or for each of its industries. Employment across Canada for the period 1961-70 increased 29.9%; any loss of jobs in some types of employment was more than offset by gains in other types. When employment is classified according to the type of industry, it becomes apparent that for all Canada the primary (agriculture, mining, fishing, etc.) and secondary (manufacturing, construction) sectors have lost jobs and the tertiary (services) sector has gained them. The growing importance of the service industries which make up the tertiary sector has been characteristic of all the regions across Canada through the 1970s and '80s.

Martin found that changes in regional employment induced by the move of industries from less profitable primary and secondary sectors to the more rewarding service sector was affected everywhere by the particular regional structure and conditions. Partly because Ontario and British Columbia had more of the fast-growing industries (i.e., employment creating) at the beginning of the period studied than the Atlantic, Quebec and Prairie regions, they still had more of those industries in 1970, the end of the period under study. However, other factors played a role, since in the Atlantic region the limited number of manufacturing firms were doing relatively well, and industries from all sectors performed much better employment-wise in British Columbia than elsewhere (Martin 1976, p. 11).

New Technology

There is an over-riding consideration which will affect the number and distribution of future employment opportunities significantly -- new technology. The most important at present is microcircuit technology. The International Labour Organization is reported to have described the silicon chip processor as the most revolutionary advance of the twentieth century, and almost as significant an invention as that of the wheel (Finn 1980). The revolution which will result from its introduction is likely to metamorphose production just as completely as did the industrial revolution. Not only the rate at which it is introduced into Canadian industry, but also the pace of its distribution across industries and across regions of the country is likely to influence the availability of employment opportunities to an important extent. Another growing industry is biotechnology (the application of organic systems and processes to manufacturing and service activities), which may produce important new drugs and foods. There are also significant contributions in genetics and other areas of cellular manipulation and enzyme technology. But Canada is less advanced in this field than some other countries and employment opportunities for the future are difficult to assess.

We have already seen that advancing technology has mechanized agriculture, forestry, mining and manufacturing, leading to declining employment opportunities in primary and secondary industry since World War II. The slack was taken up by increasing employment opportunities in the service sector. There were fewer job opportunities in such activities as farming, mining, fishing, forestry, and manufacturing; and more job openings for clerks, typists,

mail sorters, salespersons, financial consultants, and so on.
In addition, some of those persons who might otherwise have
been unemployed were put to work designing, building and
programming microelectronic systems and servicing computers.

Regional variations in the introduction and diffusion of
technological innovation are very apparent. In <u>The
Interregional Diffusion of Innovations</u> in Canada, a study
prepared for the Economic Council (Martin <u>et al</u> 1979), the
authors found the average lag (i.e., number of years behind
the leader for each innovation) in the initial adoption of
computers, BOP and electric furnaces, roof trusses, baggage
containers, special presses, and shopping centres was very
different across Canadian regions. Ontario's was the
briefest at 1.64 years, then British Columbia with 2.13, the
Prairie region and Quebec with 3.10 apiece, and the Atlantic
region with 8.08 years (p. 142, Table 9-1). The lag for
diffusion of the technical advance after its introduction was
Ontario 1.41 years, the Prairie region 2.55, Quebec 3.85,
British Columbia 4.00, and finally, the Atlantic region 6.92
(p. 147, Table 9-2). The regional factors believed to
influence the rate of technological innovation and diffusion
included the local industrial structure, degree of
urbanization, physical distance, quality of resources,
federal government initiatives and policies, and local public
and private entrepreneurship. While the authors did not
discuss employment trends, those same influences could also
be related to the number and the kind of employment
opportunities offered across the regions, in view of a
similarity between the pattern of technological diffusion and
job vacancies, as shown earlier in Figure 4.1.

New technology affects industry and related
opportunities in two ways: (1) in a competitive world, new
technology is a factor increasing productivity, generally
with the effect of raising profits and enhancing an
industry's chances of survival as a continuing source of
employment; (2) new technology may change the proportions in
which the factors of production are combined. Whether the
first effect will maintain and possibly increase the level of
employment opportunities depends upon the elasticity of
demand for the product, i.e., the increase in demand

associated with a lowering of price. The second effect will cause a decrease in employment if the innovation supplants labour.

Changes in technology are not the only factors able to increase productivity and indirectly influence employment opportunities. Other changes are higher levels of education of the work force, an extension of the hours of employment for workers, the availability of capital at lowered interest rates or through government subvention, and improvements in the quality of raw materials. Provided there is sufficient demand for the product, these influences may raise profits or alter proportions of productive factors and indirectly influence the available employment opportunities in a region.

As Martin and others have noted, urbanization affects employment opportunities significantly. The infra-structure of financial, communication and transportation services not only contributes to the efficiency of many operations but provides its own employment needs which vary positively with urban density (ECC 1977, p. 127, Table 7-4). Several fast growth service operations -- including communications, finance, insurance, real estate, and public administration as the most visible components -- are labour intensive and usually urban activities.

Urban centres also provide a local market for production. How important it is to have a near-by large market depends upon whether the product is perishable, portable, and whether it must be produced in large quantities to ensure a profit. In the case of perishability, the size of the production operation will tend to depend upon the size of the local market. Portability makes far away markets accessible. Where profitability is proportionate to the amount produced, the firm's access to capital will tend to impose limits upon the size of operation.

Almost all business today relies on borrowed money to start up and to extend operations, or for operating purposes such as financing inventories. The larger firm generally can obtain capital easily and cheaply; it may achieve a monopolistic or oligopolistic position which permits it to control the price of the product; it can more easily serve large and remote markets. Availability of capital to support large scale production enabled manufacturing in the Prairies and British Columbia to compete successfully with Ontario.

High interest rates have recently undermined production operations of most Canadian firms. Automobile production, construction activities, some types of agriculture and most small firms have been hard hit. High interest rates, inflation and escalating costs of production, as well as loss of markets, are causing many business failures across all the regions of Canada.

The small operation -- whether a case of self-employment, single proprietorship, partnership, or small corporation, is especially at risk of failure under existing conditions. Even though a market for the product may exist, the continuing imbalance between costs of production and returns from the product squeezes profits to drive all but the most hardy from the field. Consequently, except for highly qualified persons -- doctors, lawyers, skilled tradesmen, and other independent professional workers who require minimum support cost -- employment opportunities are likely to be associated increasingly with the operations of large scale firms or government which have access to sufficient supplies of capital. Many large firms are now in a holding position until inflation, escalating costs, and government policy (particularly respecting public and private investment in energy sources) become more favourable. Such conditions reduce employment opportunities temporarily, but if circumstance are not soon improved, the temporary restriction of operations may become permanent and the jobs involved will be lost forever.

The growth of multinational conglomerates also affects the availability of employment opportunities. Such conglomerates are able to operate in relation to the scale of world, rather than national costs. If labour costs are high for a specific work segment intended to be carried out in Canada, the conglomerate will move that production operation to some other part of the world where labour costs are lower. Obviously the jobs which had been scheduled for

Canada would then go elsewhere. Depending upon the labour intensity of the operation and recognizing that conglomerates are different, employment opportunities in Canada are likely to expand as multinational conglomerates become more active in Canada, and to contract as they withdraw. Moreover, since the activities of such conglomerates tend to be geographically restricted to one or a few selected locations, the employment effect may be similarly limited. For instance, the closing by Gulf Canada of the Point Tupper refinery in Nova Scotia mainly affects employment in the Atlantic provinces, even though a limited number of skilled workers may be attracted from other provinces and from other parts of te world. In this particular instance Gulf Canada's interest in developing petrochemical production from domestic oil and gas reserves and in converting Nova Scotia coal into synthetic motor fuels may provide an offsetting growth of employment opportunities.

Multinational conglomerates may also affect the quality of a country's employment opportunities by restricting operation to jobs which require only a minimum level of skill. Some conglomerates conduct basic research mainly at their home base, only providing Canadian plants with information for implementation purposes. The result may be a lack of challenging employment opportunities for highly developed skills in Canada. Even though appropriate training may be available, persons who undergo it may find that, upon completion of their education, appropriate jobs are not available in Canada.

If we contemplate what employment opportunities are likely to exist in the more remote future (until 2000 for example), we must turn to futurists such as Alvin Toffler for enlightenment (Toffler ed. 1972). The futurists promise us that employment opportunities as we know them today will have become revolutionized by the high productivity of robots and other microtechnology. Because it will no longer be necessary to work an eight hour day for self support, part-time jobs will be the order of the day. Many jobs will have been completely eliminated while others will be greatly transformed, some by moving the locus of operation from central offices to workers' homes or other local housing.

And because technology will change ever more rapidly, occupations requiring specific types of training will be rapidly out-dated. This will mean that individuals will undergo several courses of training and will work at three or more jobs during a lifetime. These trends are likely to result in substantial social change, including, perhaps, the introduction of salaries for what used to be volunteer work (possibly including housework), and, probably, some form of guaranteed minimum income.

Provincial Futures

Some factors associated with variations in regional conditions have been noted above when considering the shifts in employment resulting from change in industrial patterns of activity, provincial differences in the rate of adoption and diffusion of innovations, and factors like population density (particularly urban vs. rural), the supporting infra-structure of communication and service activities, the availability of capital, and the role of multinational conglomerates.

Agreement on the role of these factors in contributing to past productivity is not complete. A study on *Regional Disparities of Productivity and Growth in Canada* (Auer 1979) has compared aspects of labour productivity and growth in the provinces. Auer holds that the "quality of labour" is a major factor underlying differentials in labour productivity. Quality of labour, especially high educational attainment, was a factor in superior productivity in British Columbia, Alberta and Ontario, while lower educational levels in the Atlantic provinces, Quebec and Manitoba were associated with inferior output per worker. Auer's findings agree with those of *Regional Aspects of the Evolution of Canadian Employment* (Martin 1976, p. 11) that factors other than industrial structure contribute significantly to productivity in some regions, particularly in the Atlantic (where it was lower) and in British Columbia (higher). "Industrial structure made sizable contributions only in some of the Atlantic and Prairie provinces, where the potential for employment shifts out of the primary industries was still large" (p. 85).

In 1981 the Task Force on Labour Market Development in the 1980s compared the average annual per cent rates of growth of employment and the labour force by regions and found that the only region where employment growth kept up with labour force growth was the Prairies (Canada. Employment and Immigration 1981, Table 2-11, p. 27). As shown in Table 4.2, this was partly influenced by the size of the working-age population which resulted from both natural increase and net migration. These combined factors resulted in an average annual growth of the working-age population over the period 1971-80 of 3.92% in Alberta, 3.00% in British Columbia, between 2.30-2.37% in Prince Edward Island, Newfoundland and New Brunswick, 2.16% in Ontario, and below 2.00% in Nova Scotia, Quebec, Saskatchewan and Manitoba. Annual growth rates of the labour force were highest in Alberta (5.15%), followed by Newfoundland (4.21%), and British Columbia (3.99%). The lowest were in Manitoba (2.13%) and Quebec (2.61%). Labour force participation rates varied with Quebec, Manitoba and British Columbia all under 1.00%, and Newfoundland, Saskatchewan, New Brunswick and Alberta between 1.23-1.86%.

The Task Force's projections for regional employment growth in the provinces are reproduced in Table 4.3. Two sets of the projections -- A and B -- were developed by regional economists of the Canada Employment and Immigration Commission (CEIC). The third -- projection C -- represents "an alternative, more extreme view about the industrial or regional distribution of employment ... (involving) ... stronger employment growth in the West and in the Atlantic region" (pp. 47, 62). The CEIC's Projections A and B indicate "less employment growth in the East and West and more new job opportunities in the central provinces" (p. 63). These projections allow for alternative patterns of industrial growth among the provinces and related migration effects. Since industrial growth and employment may not be so closely linked in the future, there are implied assumptions about changing industry-employment ratios. Depending upon the industries involved, employment may continue to grow at a similar rate to industry or at a slower pace.

Table 4.2*   Annual Growth Rates in the Provincial Labour
             Forces and Their Components Over the Period
             1971-1980 (per cent)

Region	Labour force	Participation rate	Working-age population	Net migration[1] Inter-provincial	Net migration[1] Inter-national	Net migration[1] Total	Natural increase
Newfoundland	4.21	1.86	2.35	-0.18	.01	-0.19	2.54
Prince Edward Island	3.39	1.02	2.37	0.59	.09	0.68	1.60
Nova Scotia	3.09	1.16	1.93	0.20	.09	0.29	1.64
New Brunswick	3.61	1.31	2.30	0.46	.10	0.56	1.74
Quebec	2.61	0.95	1.66	-0.42	.10	-0.32	1.98
Ontario	3.19	1.03	2.16	-0.08	.53	0.45	1.71
Manitoba	2.13	0.96	1.17	-0.72	.36	-0.36	1.53
Saskatchewan	2.78	1.44	1.34	-0.61	.05	-0.56	1.90
Alberta	5.15	1.23	3.92	1.16	.48	1.64	2.28
British Columbia	3.99	0.99	3.00	0.78	.48	1.26	1.74
Canada	3.25	1.08	2.17	--	.33	.33	1.84

[1] Annual average net adult migration over 1971-80 divided by mid-period adult population.

Source: Labour force and participation rate data based on Statistics Canada, Labour Force Survey. Net migration data based on Statistics Canada, International and Interprovincial Migration in Canada and Population: Revised Annual Estimates of Population, by Sex and Age, for Canada and the Provinces, 1971-1976.

* Reproduced from Canada. Employment and Immigration Canada. Labour Market Development in the 1980's. Report of the Task Force on Labour Market Development -- (The Dodge Report). Ottawa: Supply and Services Canada, 1981, Table 2-12, p. 28.

Table 4.3* Employment Growth by Provinces
(average annual per cent rates of growth)

	1973-79	1980-85 CEIC Regional Projection		1980-85 Alternative Regional Projection
		A	B	C
Newfoundland	3.2	1.5	1.1	4.0
Prince Edward Island	3.9	1.4	1.0	2.1
Nova Scotia	2.8	1.9	1.7	2.6
New Brunswick	2.8	2.2	1.9	1.8
Quebec	2.4	1.7	1.5	1.4.
Ontario	3.1	2.0	1.6	1.4
Manitoba	2.3	1.5	0.9	2.1
Saskatchewan	3.1	2.3	2.0	2.9
Alberta	5.5	4.4	4.1	5.1
British Columbia	3.9	2.5	2.2	3.1
Total	3.2	2.2	1.9	2.2

Source: Historical data based on Statistics Canada, Labour Force Survey. Projections developed by Task Force.

* Reproduced from Canada. Employment and Immigration Canada. Labour Market Development in the 1980's. Report of the Task Force on Labour Market Development - (the Dodge Report). Ottawa: Supply and Services Canada, 1981, Table 4-12, p. 63.

Associated with shifts in employment there may be spin-off effects upon regional income distribution which will be significant. The salaries of workers who continue in their jobs in areas of industrial growth are likely to be as high (and probably higher in real terms) as at present. But the income lost by workers displaced by microtechnology and other labour-saving developments may more than offset the gains of workers still on the job. Economic growth could begin in consciously selected industries or regions as provinces with new-found wealth strive to support their unemployed populations. Interprovincial migration (Tables 4.4 and 4.5) has been strongly affected in the past by interregional differentials in salaries and wages (R.M. McInnis 1969, and others). In future, migration also may be affected by regional transfer arrangements (or their inadequacy) for unemployment insurance, welfare support, health plans and other benefits usually considered subsidiary to income. R.G. Bodkin (1981) has suggested that schemes for guaranteed incomes may become economically viable and politically important. They could partly replace earned incomes as an attraction for migrants.

Table 4.4*   Interprovincial Migration Flows**
               (annual average '000)

	In-migration 1961-71	In-migration 1971-80	Out-migration 1961-71	Out-migration 1971-80	Net migration 1961-71	Net migration 1971-80
Newfoundland	7.7	11.4	11.1	12.5	-3.5	-1.1
Prince Edward Island	3.7	4.6	4.3	3.9	-0.6	0.7
Nova Scotia	22.1	24.0	26.5	22.7	-4.4	1.3
New Brunswick	18.5	20.9	23.0	18.4	-4.5	2.5
Quebec	41.4	32.2	55.7	56.6	-14.3	-24.4
Ontario	104.2	95.7	80.7	102.7	23.6	-7.0
Manitoba	27.4	27.0	33.8	34.5	-6.4	-7.5
Saskatchewan	22.8	26.6	35.2	29.4	-12.4	-2.8
Alberta	52.0	81.5	49.0	61.7	3.0	19.8
British Columbia	62.0	73.7	42.7	54.8	19.3	18.9

**For all adults and children

Source: Based on Statistics Canada, International and Interprovincial Migration in Canada.
*Reproduced from Canada. Employment and Immigration Canada. Labour Market Development in the 1980's.
Report of the Task Force on Labour Market Development (The Dodge Report). Ottawa: Supply and
Services Canada, 1981. Table 2-13, p. 29.

Table 4.5*   Interprovincial Net Migration of Children and Adults (annual averages, '000)

	NFLD	PEI	NS	NB	QUE	ONT	MAN	SASK	ALTA	BC
1961-66	-3.0	-0.6	-5.4	-5.1	-4.0	17.1	-4.7	-8.4	-0.4	15.5
1966-71	-3.9	-0.6	-3.3	-3.9	-24.5	30.1	-8.1	-16.3	6.4	23.0
1971-76	-0.4	0.8	2.3	3.4	-15.5	-7.7	-5.4	-8.2	11.7	18.5
1976-77	-1.4	1.0	0.2	2.6	-23.0	-8.0	-4.2	6.8	25.3	2.1
1977-78	-2.6	0.7	0.7	1.9	-46.9	10.1	-7.2	2.0	25.8	15.7
1978-79	-1.9	-0.1	1.4	1.1	-32.1	-8.1	-10.9	1.7	30.4	20.1
1979-80	-1.0	0.4	-1.1	0.6	-31.3	-19.6	-15.9	-0.4	30.9	39.4
1980-85										
CEIC Regional Projection										
Alternative A	-9.5	-0.8	0.1	0.0	-11.3	-18.3	-6.8	3.5	34.9	8.2
Alternative B	-8.0	-0.3	0.7	0.8	-6.1	-24.3	-7.7	3.1	32.3	9.5
Alternative projection	2.4	0.2	4.5	-2.5	-32.0	-58.1	0.8	8.1	50.9	25.8

Note: Historical data refer to census year, i.e. year beginning June 1 of year T and ending May 31 of Year T+1.

Source: Historical data based on Statistics Canada, *International and Interprovincial Migration in Canada*. Projections developed by Task Force.

*Reproduced from Canada. Employment and Immigration Canada. *Labour Market Development in the 1980's. Report of the Task Force on Labour Market Development* (The Dodge Report). Ottawa: Supply and Services Canada, 1981. Table 4-13, p. 64.

The migration projections indicate large movements out of Ontario and Quebec, into Alberta and British Columbia, and smaller streams heading for Saskatchewan, Nova Scotia, and possibly Manitoba. New Brunswick may show little growth or even lose population from migration. The substantial differences among the sizes of alternative projections for migration reflect the wide range of expectations respecting regional industrial growth, changing industry-employment ratios, and the ability of employment to keep abreast of future regional population and labour force growth.

While industrial growth and prosperity probably will be greatest in those provinces where the most innovative processes have been adopted, the rate at which the industry-employment ratio will change will relate partly to the adaptability of existing industry. Heavy industries like gas and oil in Alberta, offshore Nova Scotia and Newfoundland, as well as iron and steel in Ontario and Quebec have low industry-employment ratios because they are already well advanced in labour-saving technologies. By applying the new methods to manufactures like cars, combines, and rail and subway equipment, as well as to industries like textiles and shoe-making with higher industry-employment ratios, Ontario and Quebec, in particular, could become more competitive on world markets. Investment in the traditionally high employment industries like textiles and boots and shoes is expected to be substantial. For instance, over the rest of the '80s new high speed machinery and computerized control, combined with modernization of techniques for making, spinning, weaving and finishing textiles, are all in view.

Of course, new technology does not project provincial futures reliably: markets for the products are even more important. Future forestry in British Columbia, for instance, will be largely determined by the size of U.S. demand for lumber and pulp and paper products, as well as the needs of the provincial construction industry which is the biggest employer in the province. Quebec and New Brunswick production of pulp and paper will be similarly discouraged if world demand declines. Mining also, in British Columbia, Ontario and Quebec, and agriculture in the Prairies, depends upon world markets, particularly those of the United States.

Alberta industry will be important to Canada if the oil and gas activities resume at their earlier levels and support a host of related operations. But a decline in the market and prices for petroleum products has led to lower profits and dampened prospects for the industry's growth. As a result, oil explorations and petroleum production in Alberta, the Northwest Territories, and offshore operations in Newfoundland and Nova Scotia will provide less employment than expected. Alberta companies may restrict petroleum production to the "old" oil wells -- those which were discovered before 1974; a multi-billion dollar oil sand project which was put on "hold" in late 1980 may never get off the ground. Oil off the shores of Newfoundland and Nova Scotia will not be developed as vigorously as expected; some projects may close down.

The future promises a boom in high technology, particularly in Toronto, Ottawa and Montreal, and telecommunications development in Montreal and Saskatoon. These activities have led to world wide marketing of computers, telecommunications, microelectronics, software and other such products, in competition with major competitors such as Japan and the United States. Meantime they improved productivity in other Canadian industries.

But new technology's impact on the employment market is worrisome. Planning and retraining and reassignment of workers to other production areas can help, but under conditions currently prevailing across Canada, companies are forced to introduce such cost-cutting techniques to survive, so that there is little room for the luxury of planned adjustment. Employment could be adversely affected for years. And areas, like Ontario, which have profited most from superior production methods in the past, may suffer from severe unemployment in the foreseeable future. Those provinces with large industrial sectors in activities which can easily adapt to innovations are likely to show more rapid increases in productivity and industrial growth, but at the expense of reduced employment. Regions with greatest prosperity may also become regions of high unemployment for some time to come.

Which regions will experience the greatest prosperity over the remaining years of the century? This is difficult to foresee although the future of the provinces will be conditioned in part by present and past regional trends. However, developments inside and outside Canada affecting markets for Canadian products, the world availability of resources (particularly food, energy, and other products in limited supply), the extent to which cartels like the Organization of Petroleum Exporting Countries can control supplies and prices of essential commodities; and other occurrences such as outbreak of war, over which Canada has little or no control, will be at least as important influences on future national and regional prosperity.

Implications for Employment Opportunities, Selected Groups

The likely changes which will occur in productive activity in Canada over future years are already under way. Inflation and high interest rates are pushing us to cut production costs and to increase productivity. Two present responses -- the amalgamation of firms into larger units until they achieve the vast size of multinational conglomerates, and the adoption of innovative, labour-replacing technology -- may only be beginning. Futurists predict that innovations may come about so rapidly that mankind may attempt to control the rate of change through licensing or regulating the implementation of innovations in order to allow for a period of adjustment (Toffler 1970).

At the same time the transition from the primary and secondary industries will likely continue, particularly in the corridor from Montreal to Windsor and in urban areas in British Columbia, the Prairies and the Atlantic provinces. Workers displaced by increasingly productive mechanical operations will seek out jobs where they are most available -- and that will be in the service industries. But innovative labour-saving technology will be increasingly introduced to those industries as well. What is this likely to mean for the average Canadian worker, and for those special groups which experience some degree of discrimination in the labour market today?

It is not too difficult to guess some of the specific jobs which will have a good future. First will be those jobs related to computer operations. They will require the ability to manipulate associated software. There will be a strong demand for electrical and electronic engineers, technologists, technicians, systems analysts, senior analysts, senior programers, technical programers, system programers, data processors, data encoders, etc. There will also be a need for persons who are knowledgeable about graphics, telecommunications, hardware, training, and sales related to different informatics applications and computer -- or microprocessor -- based systems (Menzies 1981, p. 83). And in the biotechnological field there will be a need for trained biologists, geneticists, physicists, chemists, agrarian specialists and oceanographers who will work to improve the quality of life and to extend life-supporting production of foods, drugs, and other scarce substances from little explored sources.

There are problems in forecasting the future for jobs currently important in the Canadian economy, since so much depends upon the strength of foreign competition and decisions which are taken by both Canada and other countries respecting foreign trade. Otherwise, there are certainly underlying trends in our society which suggest some characteristics of the future interface between the job market and the labour force. The greater mechanization of all forms of industry displaces labour of relatively unskilled persons, but also tends to increase the demand for highly educated and highly skilled persons who can manipulate and improve the system. Microelectronic advancements and other transformations are by no means complete, and biotechnological applications are just beginning.

Even in primary and secondary industry productivity may be increased through additional computer technology. Walter Hirsh (Versatile Farm Equipment) indicated that eventually the computer could monitor all farm operations, relate them to each other and control machines. Ultimately an onboard computer could replace the driver who will be required in the initial stages of development. It will be some time before robots take over crop planting and harvesting, even though computer technology has been adapted to irrigation problems. Sensing of problems and the initiation of appropriate actions and reactions still must be improved before computers make their full contribution to productivity in some sectors of industry but it is easier than in some of the service functions. When highly developed technology does infiltrate the service industries more completely there will be a large-scale displacement of labour, since it is the chief sector presently offering high employment opportunities. The social implications are not yet completely understood, but one effect could be a greater prevalence of employment-sharing, i.e., worksharing, jobsharing, or part-time employment, particularly if changes are made to provide health coverage and other fringe benefits to such workers (Meltz et al. 1981, Chapter 5).

Another trend affecting employment opportunities and job requirements is the down-grading, both by society as a whole and by its youthful age groups in particular, of the value of traditional types of education and training, including that associated with universities. The opting out of education by young people, especially during the latter half of the '70s, has been well publicized. Although there has been a reversal of this trend over the last few years, the effects of dropping out in the '70s will remain for that age group. The need for trained workers like biologists, geneticists and mathematicians (for example) may not be met over the immediate future.

Over the next few years a shortage of skilled trades workers like tool and die makers, is also imminent unless either more apprenticeship programs are developed or a substantial number of immigrants with these skills enter Canada. However, "many of the skills that pose major problems in Canada seem, in fact, to be in demand throughout the industrialized world. Accordingly, it must be recognized that the remedial value of immigration is limited" (Betcherman 1982, p. 69).

As the baby boom generation ages, fewer new entrants will enter the job market, so that the problem of unemployment may ease somewhat. Estimates by David K. Foot are that new entrants into the job market are likely to occur at a rate of 2.1% or more each year throughout the '80s which could mean that over 2.25 million new jobs would be needed, requiring "a real output growth rate averaging 3.7 per cent per annum over the decade" (Foot 1982, p. 214). While the projections in Table 4.6 which are the basis of reference for this chapter suggest a rate of growth under 2%, it is clear that the problem of providing employment is likely to remain difficult for some years to come. Unless immigration is restricted, job-seekers from other parts of the world could exacerbate the problem.

Table 4.6 Percentage Distribution of Population by Three Main Age Groups Medium Projection for Canada, Selected Years

Assumptions

Mortality: Assumes that changes between 1971-1991 will be 1.5 times changes in 1951-71, and that changes between 1991-2011 will be .75 times changes in 1951-71.

Fertility: Assumes some increase from the calculated level of 1,896 children per 1000 wolmen in 1974 to a level of 2,100 children by 1984 and thereafter.

Net Migration: Assumed at 120,000 per annum.

Age Group	1976	1981	1991	2001	2011	2021	2031	2041	2051
			THOUSANDS OF POPULATION						
0-19	35.8	32.5	30.4	29.4	26.9	26.6	26.0	25.6	25.9
20-64	55.4	58.1	58.7	58.6	60.0	57.2	54.8	55.8	55.3
65 +	8.7	9.5	11.0	12.0	13.1	16.2	19.2	18.6	18.7

Source: Based on data in Frank T. Denton, Christine H. Feaver and Byron G. Spencer, The Future Population and Labour Force of Canada: Projections to the Year 2051. A study prepared for the Economic Council of Canada. Hull, Quebec: Canadian Government Publishing Centre, 1980. Chapters 4 and 5.

If present low levels of fertility persist in Canada, and assuming that immigration has not augmented the effects of natural increase upon population growth, by the year 2001 there may be a top-heavy proportion of older workers in the labour force and an insufficient number of workers in the more junior ranks. Of the two effects, the aging of the labour force is likely to be the more troublesome since, so far as employment is concerned, reduction of the number of workers at younger ages may be offset by the employment-reducing impact of technological advance. Questions of seniority, progress through the ranks of industry, and financial responsibility for the needs of dependent segments of the population -- especially those 65 and over -- will then become pressing social issues (Foot 1982, Chapter 4; Stone 1977).

The economic effects of changes in age and sex groups of the population have been discussed by a number of writers (Easterlin 1978, 1968; Keyfitz 1971, 1972, 1973 and others). An Easterlin-Wachter model (Easterlin 1978) traced the substitution and complementarity effects likely to be associated with changes in employment opportunities for sex and age groups 15-29 and 30-64 as a consequence of long swings in the patterns of aggregate demand for, and supply of, labour. The authors suggested that before World War II private investment booms of about 15 to 20 years in duration generated a major swing in the total demand for labour which was independent of the supply of labour available. After the War, demand for labour remained high as a result of monetary-fiscal policy. Swings in labour supply reflected the effects of earlier birth rates and were largely independent of demand for labour. The Easterlin-Wachter model then introduced the effects of shifts in the relative scarcity of young adults under two assumptions: (1) that the working age population consists only of younger and older males, and (2) that the working age population consists of both younger and older males and females. The effects upon wages, unemployment rates, occupational mobility and labour force participation were then analyzed, assuming long swings of perhaps 35 to 40 years in aggregate demand and labour supply.

Competition among the generation now passing through the young to middle working ages reduces their competitive position. Although nominally their wages have increased, in real terms they have been reduced; their occupational mobility is not so great as formerly; and their unemployment rates have increased. These trends may continue until at least 2011, after which time the maximum proportions in the 20 to 64 age group will have been reached and the situation will adjust to continuing growth in the 65+ ages until at least 2031. After that time the proportions of population in the older and working ages may stabilize or even decline slightly. However, until 2031, the distribution of ages within the work force will continue to be skewed upwards. As this occurs, the proportion of younger people in the labour force will decrease and their growing relative scarcity will gradually improve their competitive position in the labour market. Other things being equal, the wages and occupational mobility of younger workers will be likely to improve and their unemployment rates should decline. Lower levels of fertility and net migration now occurring in Canada could advance these trends.

If we consider the future job outlooks by sex the situation becomes more complicated. Although the same influences as outlined above will hold generally, the effect upon women workers will be modified by their lower rate of labour force participation (now rising) as compared with men; by selectivity of their job opportunities; by women's substitutability for, or complementarity with, male workers; and by the substitutability of age groups within their own ranks. When there is an abundance of young persons as is happening now, the younger females will compete with young males for jobs. If there is a preference for male workers over much of the labour market, the male applicants rather than the females will get the jobs. Wages for young females may then decline, and unemployment rates go up more for young women than for young men. These difficulties in finding jobs may be masked, for those who spend months looking for jobs without success may be discouraged from continuing the search, and so become drop-outs.

Because the young age group generally is at a

disadvantage respecting wages, so that family income is relatively low when only the husbands work, labour force participation by younger married women will rise out of necessity rather than preference to work outside of the home. Older females are in even more difficult straits since they generally substitute for the already disadvantaged younger women in the work force. When younger women are plentiful or their rate of labour force participation rises, the opportunities for older women shrink. However, older women already established in their jobs may not be disadvantaged if their numbers are in short supply and/or they are protected by seniority rights.

If we pursue the effect of family income (i.e., of both husband and wife) on women's labour force participation, it is likely that as wages and occupational mobility of younger men go up, the labour force participation of their wives may decline (presumably because these women prefer leisure or childbearing). An even stronger inverse relationship is likely to exist between income of older men and the labour force role of older women, since labour force participation of women declines with age (women's labour force participation in 1981 was 9.8% for women 15-20; 73.0% for ages 20-24; 62.7% for ages 25-54; and 14.8% for women 55 and over (Canada. Statistics Canada 1982, pp. 196-8). Applying these modifications to projected population in Canada, and assuming that the sex ratio at different ages is approximately that for 1981, we can postulate that until about 2011 labour force participation of younger women may increase; their real wages are likely to decline; and their unemployment rates may rise. Older women will be less able to compete as substitutes for younger women.

The type of job opportunity open to women is also a factor. Women have tended to be concentrated in teaching, nursing, sales and certain clerical occupations, where they typically cluster at the bottom of the income pyramid. Since women work mostly in service activities they are even more likely than men to be displaced by technological advances in the coming years. Canada Manpower and Immigration's campaign to recruit more women into training for jobs traditionally filled by men should help offset these dampening influences upon women's employment opportunities.

After the year 2011 younger persons -- both males and females -- may again be in short supply. The labour force balance between the sexes will be related to rates of labour force participation which will probably depend upon family income and cost-of-living increases. If family incomes grow faster, young women's labour force participation could decline, even though wages and occupational mobility for younger women would likely be improving. In that case, older females would substitute for younger women in the labour market and achieve real gains in wages. On the other hand, if cost-of-living forces are more dominant, younger females may have higher labour force participation rates, affecting older women adversely respecting job opportunities, wages and unemployment rates.

These trends apply for Canada as a whole. Regional differences would be very difficult to project even twenty years ahead. Some inkling of their pattern may be gleaned from labour force participation rates for men and women by province in 1981, as given in Table 4.7. The rates shown in that table are highest for Alberta and lowest in Newfoundland. Possibly the differentials will close somewhat in future years, depending upon the strength of regional structure and local influences, as well as government policy.

Table 4.7   Labour Force Participation by Sex, For Canadian Provinces in 1981

Province	Rate of Participation	
	Male	Female
Newfoundland	67.4	38.5
Prince Edward Island	71.4	47.2
Nova Scotia	71.1	45.3
New Brunswick	69.9	44.0
Quebec	76.1	47.0
Ontario	80.5	55.6
Manitoba	78.4	52.2
Saskatchewan	78.7	48.3
Alberta	84.7	58.5
British Columbia	77.9	51.9
Canada	78.3	51.6

Source: Canada. Statistics Canada. Historical Labour Force Statistics 1981 -- actual data, seasonal factors, seasonally adjusted data. Ottawa: Minister of Supply and Services, Canada, 1982. Cat. 71-201 Annual.

While projecting implications for opportunity for males and females across Canada into the first part of the twenty-first century obviously leaves much to be desired, projecting opportunities for selected ethnic populations is even more hazardous. However, some general observations can be made about the future of immigrants in the job market.

Immigration policy has been related to manpower needs over most of Canada's history. From Confederation until after World War I immigration recruitment emphasized settlers who would cultivate the land, particularly the rich wheat land in the Prairies. Immigration policy was very selective, seeking not only persons who would fill recognized occupational needs but also particular ethnic characteristics. For many years highest preferences were for persons from Great Britain and the United States and other countries of northwestern Europe. Gentlemen's agreements, the establishment of quotas, high head taxes on new immigrants, and the requirement that the immigrant should travel directly to Canada from his country of origin, effectively restricted the immigration of Asiatic races and other coloured persons considered to be undesirable immigrants (Macleod 1967, pp. 121-140).

After World War II, the policy towards immigrants changed radically, although it was still married to occupational needs. Where those needs had been perceived earlier as relating primarily to land cultivation, in the postwar years they included broader requirements. Annual surveys of job needs resulted in attempts to recruit immigrants capable of meeting these needs. There were still some attempts to recruit farmers, but attention shifted to finding skilled tradesmen for construction, mining, forestry, manufacturing and the expanding service industries. More recent immigrants have consequently filled a wide range of occupations. They have also come from more varied backgrounds. Some were displaced from their homelands during the war; others were from southeastern Europe where birthrates and natural increase of population remained high during the first decade after the war; and some still came from the previously preferred sources. As it became apparent that Canada's prosperity depended upon persons for key jobs, immigration policy became more and more liberal, welcoming immigrants from sources such as India, Pakistan and the Caribbean.

The 1966 review of immigration policy led to more open migration from all lands, irrespective of race, colour, or the characteristics which had been used earlier to limit immigration. The new policy stressed training, education and experience, as well as knowledge of one of the official languages, English and French. Immigrants not otherwise admissable could often immigrate under the family or assisted relatives schemes (Canada. Manpower and Immigration 1974, Chapter 2). As the economic environment deteriorated, suitability for work on a job which could not be filled by Canadians began to increase in importance (Macleod 1967, pp. 265-286). Indications are that this emphasis will continue throughout the '80s, and that immigration levels will be partly determined by the estimated natural increase in Canada for each year, and by the gross immigration considered necessary to offset emigration and to support natural increase in order to achieve the annual target rate of growth for the total population. In recent years the gross immigration level has been declining, partly because workers in Canada are given preference in job allocations and partly because the target rates of growth have been low. Factors contributing to a substantial growth in labour force participation in Canada -- higher participation by women than has ever occurred before, and the baby boom's progress into the early and middle ages of the labour force -- will soon stabilize. If fertility levels remain low, immigration may then become the chief element in maintaining Canada's population growth. However, it is not clear that, in the more remote future, a sufficient supply of immigrants will enter to meet either population or labour force goals.

Estimates of the contribution of net immigration and domestic sources to the labour force over selected periods since 1951 indicate that net immigration's contribution has fallen from 1% to 0.2% in terms of the average annual per cent rate of growth for 1951-56 and 1976-79. The total labour force grew by 2.1% in 1951 and 3.0% in 1976-79 (Canada. Employment and Immigration Canada 1981, p. 21).

Employment opportunities for immigrants in the past have been associated with whatever industries were expanding at the time of the immigrants' arrival in Canada. The Chinese around the turn of the century obtained jobs building the railroad; the European immigrants in the early 1900's and after World War I farmed the new wheat lands; after World war II the refugees, assisted and independent immigrants, found jobs in a wide variety of occupations, but particularly manufacturing and the service industries (Macleod 1967). Also a substantial number of highly skilled and professional immigrants filled many needs. According to a survey done in 1978 for the Department of Manpower and Immigration, "only 27 per cent of the skilled labour force was born in Canada" (ECC 1982, p. 42). Immigration is unlikely to play as significant a role as it has in the past in meeting skill shortages because supplies of outside manpower are drying up, so that "the focus must be on Canada's domestic capability to develop needed skills" (p. 46).

It is likely that the service industries and the rapidly growing automated technology activities will be prime sources for employment of immigrants entering Canada to the end of this century. Job and immigration trends for the next century are not yet predictable.

Some characteristics of immigrants to Canada were described in a 1971 Census Study (Richmond and Kalbach 1980, pp. 103-20). Immigrant men and women had higher labour force participation rates and higher incomes (except for men and women aged 15-24) than their counterparts in the native-born Canadian population. Variability in ethnic group median incomes declined in relation to length of residence and was related to specific ethnic origin groups. Incomes were highest for immigrants from the British Isles, northern and western Europe, then the French, with immigrants from other parts of the world getting lowest incomes. New immigrants were more likely to be wage earners than were the native born, but given time, inclined more towards becoming employers and working on their own account. Percentages of males working as employers or on their own account were highest for Jewish (25.5%), followed by immigrants from northern and western Europe, central and eastern Europe and Asian countries. French and British followed, between 10-11% (p. 293).

Conclusions

This chapter has outlined some changes in the Canadian economy which are likely to influence employment and educational development in Canada. But the bridge between the economy and education has not yet been put into place. The question needs to be asked: How will the economic trends indicated above affect the need for, or the ability to supply education in the future?

Obviously, inflation and associated increases in salaries of teachers and other educational personnel will seriously hinder educational progress, just as they are undermining other industries in the economy. The burgeoning costs attendant upon inflation -- largely arising out of the labour intensive aspect of education -- force educational bodies to increase fees and to cut back on many desirable activities and programs in order to reduce the level of expenditures. It seems as though "Nothing short of radical educational surgery can stop these inexorable cost increases" (Coombs 1981, p. 13). At the same time, inflation and high interest rates affect the costs of student loans so that fewer persons may enter or complete university or skilled training programs offered at community colleges or other advanced training centres. Governments cut back educational grants in order to use existing resources more efficiently, or to redirect funds to other areas (health) where the public make heavier political demands. Or the individual taxpayer simply contributes less because of unemployment or moves to housing with a lower assessment value.

Secondly, the changes which have occurred over the last five years or so may reflect the worth which education currently enjoys in the eyes of the public. Education has suffered from a loss of prestige, partly because its graduates experience difficulty obtaining employment, and partly because inflation has eroded the salary advantages which formerly favoured the educated worker. The prestige of education, and the bargaining power of educators and graduates will continue to soften, but it must be noted that less education is not an economic advantage (Nediger 1981). Clearly some kinds of education or training are better than others. If highly qualified persons fail to enter teaching and research, the loss cannot be recouped within a short period of years.

Fortunately, the rapid growth of the service industries, including health and communication, will stimulate education to some extent. Law, finance, insurance, medicine, and certain other activities which are among the most financially rewarding in society, increase the demand for appropriate programs. Indeed, these pursuits could become overcrowded (as seems to be the case for lawyers and doctors in Ontario), so that expansion of educational facilities offering the appropriate training programs might not be realistic.

There will undoubtedly be a continuing and perhaps increased demand for education to support technological innovation. We can anticipate the need for highly skilled persons to develop and modify all the new techologies. The demand will be associated with the growth of the new communications technology, with biotechnology and with anticipated megaprojects in oil, gas, petrochemical products, electricity, mining and aerospace. The extent to which the demand for related training will be reflected in provinces and regions across Canada will depend partly upon government policy and grants, but will also reflect regional structure and conditions, including the reputation and diversity of existing educational institutions. The degree of urbanization, physical distance from libraries and other supporting facilities, and the attitude towards innovation and change in the local area are all likely to be factors influencing educational improvements.

Technological advance is also likely to affect education. Because of the rapidity of change, career opportunities which now exist may be completely irrelevant to society's future needs. Such developments may mean that individuals will be called upon to train and retrain for several careers during their lifetime. Consequently, education will no longer be a process completed in early adulthood. Programs and options will need to be available to persons of all ages, at all times (Gelpi 1979). Part-time and after-hours education is going to be an increasing need to facilitate the individual's adaptation to changing life situations.

Increases in productivity due to technical innovations should give greater financial security to the firms which adopt them. Increased profits will likely lead to further improvements and a spin-off demand for more persons with the ability to develop other technical improvements. As progress in technology is made, demand for highly educated persons can be expected to intensify, and the prestige of education may rise again. There is likely to be a mutual reinforcement for high levels of education which is based upon the productive contributions of the graduates and the employers' desire to extend them. The prospects for workers who have only low or middle levels of education are less sanguine. Persons in those categories are in danger of having many of their functions replaced eventually by robots.

Finally, the need to encourage the ability of workers to adapt to changing situations merits underlining, since adjustment to rapid shifts in technology and related job needs will be a priority. On these grounds, a case can be made for continuing support of liberal arts education since it may enable its recipient to grasp more fully the directions of social and economic change and to develop a life style more amenable to society's emergent needs.

REFERENCES

Auer, Ludwig. Regional Disparities of Productivity and Growth in Canada, a study prepared for the Economic Council of Canada (Hull: Canadian Government Publishing Centre, 1979).

Betcherman, Gordon. Meeting Skill Requirements, report of the human resources survey, a study prepared for the Economic Council of Canada (Ottawa: Canadian Government Publications Centre, 1982).

Bodkin, R.G. "The Challenge of Inflation and Unemployment in Canada during the 1980's: Would a Tax-Based Incomes Policy Help?" Canadian Public Policy VII Supplement (April 1981) 204-214.

Canada. Deparment of Finance. Economic Development for Canada in the 1980s, report of the ad-hoc committee of Cabinet Ministers (Ottawa: Department of Finance, 1981).

.... Economic Review (Ottawa: Canadian Government Publishing Centre, 1980, 1981, and 1982).

Canada. Employment and Immigration Canada. Annual Report to Parliament on Immigration Levels (Ottawa: Employment and Immigration Canada, 1980 and 1981).

.... Immigration and Demographic Policy Group. 1980 Immigration Statistics, Canada (Ottawa: Minister of Supply and Services Canada, 1982).

Canada. Employment and Immigration Canada. Labour Market Development in the 1980s, report of the Task Force on Labour Market Development (the Dodge Report) (Ottawa: Supply and Services Canada, 1981).

Canada. Manpower and Immigration. Immigration and Population Statistics, Canadian Immigration and Population Study (part of the Green Paper) (Ottawa: Information Canada, 1974).

Canada. Manpower and Immigration. *2. The Immigraton Program*, Canadian Immigration and Population Study (part of the Green Paper) (Ottawa: Information Canada, 1974a).

Canada. Statistics Canada, Labour Division. *Annual Report on Job Vacancies 1978* (Ottawa: Statistics Canada, 1979), Cat. 71-203.

Canada. Statistics Canada. *Canadian Statistical Review* (Ottawa: Minister of Supply and Services Canada, Dec. 1982 and Jan. 1983).

.... Labour Force Survey Group. *Historical Labour Force Statistics, 1981 -- Actual Data, Seasonal Factors, Seasonally Adjusted Data* (Ottawa: Minister of Supply and Services Canada, 1982), Cat. 71-201 Annual.

Coombs, Philip H. *Future Critical World Issues in Education: A Provisional Report of Findings* (Essex, U.S.A.: International Council for Educational Development, 1981).

Copithorne, L. *Natural Resources and Regional Disparities*, a study prepared for the Economic Council of Canada (Hull: Canadian Government Publishing Centre, 1979).

Denton, Frank T., Christine H. Feaver and Byron G. Spencer. *The Future Population and Labour Force of Canada: Projections to the Year 2051*, a study prepared for the Economic Council of Canada (Hull: Canadian Government Publishing Centre, 1980).

Easterlin, Richard A. *Population Labour Force and Long Swings in Economic Growth* (New York: Columbia University Press, 1968).

.... "What will 1984 be like? Socioeconomic Implications of Recent Twists in Age Structure", *Demography* 15:4, 1978, 397-432.

Economic Council of Canada. *A Climate of Uncertainty*, Seventeenth Annual Review (Hull: Minister of Supply and Services Canada, 1980).

.... In Short Supply, Jobs and Skills in the 1980s (Ottawa: Canadian Government Publishing Centre, 1982).

.... Lean Times, Policies and Constraints, Nineteenth Annual Review (Ottawa: Minister of Supply and Services Canada, 1982).

.... Living Together, A Study of Regional Disparities (Hull:Canadian Government Publishing Centre, 1977).

.... Room to Manoeuvre, Eighteenth Annual Review (Hull: Minister of Supply and Services Canada, 1981).

Finn, Ed. "We're careening into the computer age -- but without a plan", Toronto Star, February 17, 1980.

Foot, David K. Canada's Population Outlook: Demographic Futures and Economic Challenges, Canadian Institute for Economic Policy Series (Toronto: James Lorimer & Co., 1982).

Gelpi, Ettore. "Education and Later Life in Industrial Society", Chapter 8 in A Future for Lifelong Education, Volume 1: Lifelong Education: principles, policies and practices, Manchester Monographs 13 (Manchester: Department of Adult and Higher Education, the University of Manchester, 1979).

Keyfitz, Nathan. "Individual Mobility in a Stationary Population", Population Studies 27 (2), 1973, 335-52.

.... "On the Momentum of Population Growth", Demography 8, 1971, 71-80.

.... "Population Waves" in T.N.E. Greville (ed.) Population Dynamics (New York: Academic Press, 1972).

Macleod, Betty Robinson. A History of Canadian Economic Development with Special Reference to Immigration, Ph.D. thesis (Durham, N.C.: Duke University. University Microfilms 68-5225, 1967).

Martin, Fernand. *Regional Aspects of the Evolution of Canadian Employment*, a study prepared for the Economic Council of Canada, with the assistance of Richard Beaudry (Ottawa: Information Canada, 1976).

Martin, F., N. Swan, I. Banks, G. Barker, and R. Beaudry. *The Interregional Diffusion of Innovations in Canada*, a study prepared for the Economic Council of Canada (Hull: Canadian Government Publishing Centre, 1979).

McInnis, R.M. "Provincial Migration and Differential Economic Opportunity", Chapter 5 in L.O. Stone (ed.), *Migration in Canada*. 1961 Census Monograph (Ottawa: Queen's Printer, 1969).

Meltz, Noah M., Frank Reid and Gerald S. Swartz. *Sharing the Work: an analysis of the issues in worksharing and jobsharing* (Toronto: University of Toronto Press, 1981).

Menzies, Heather. *Women and the Chip* (Montreal: The Institute for Research on Public Policy, 1981).

Nediger, W.G. "The Impact of Collective Bargaining on Financial Gains and Management Rights in Canadian Education" (ERIC Clearinghouse on Educational Management, 1981).

Richmond, Anthony H. and Warren E. Kalbach. *Factors in the Adjustment of Immigrants and Their Descendants*, 1971 Census Analytical Study prepared for Statistics Canada (Ottawa: Minister of Supply and Services Canada, 1980).

Stone, Leroy O. "Employment Opportunity and the Achievement of Adequate Old-Age Income for the Baby Boom Generation", in B.T. Wigdor (ed.), *Canadian Gerontolical Collection I Selected Papers* (Toronto: Canadian Association of Gerontology, 1977).

Toffler, Alfred. *Future Shock* (New York: Random House, 1970).

.... (ed.) *The Futurists* (Toronto: Random House, 1972).

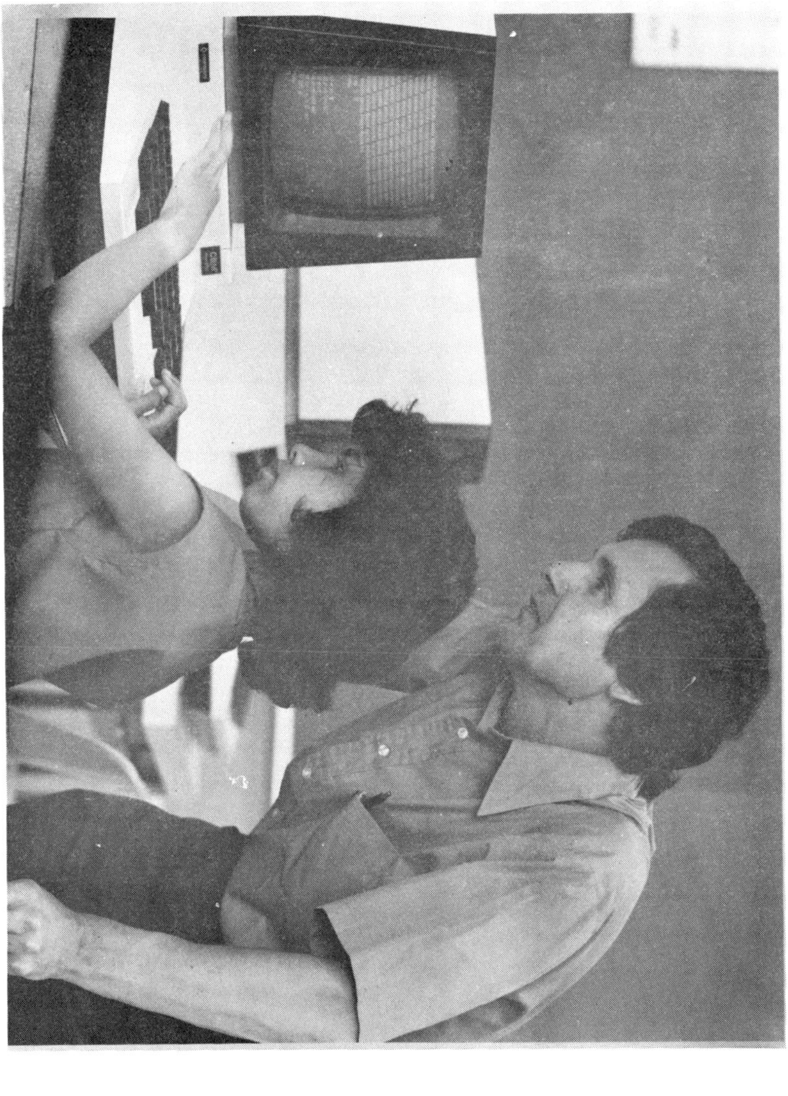

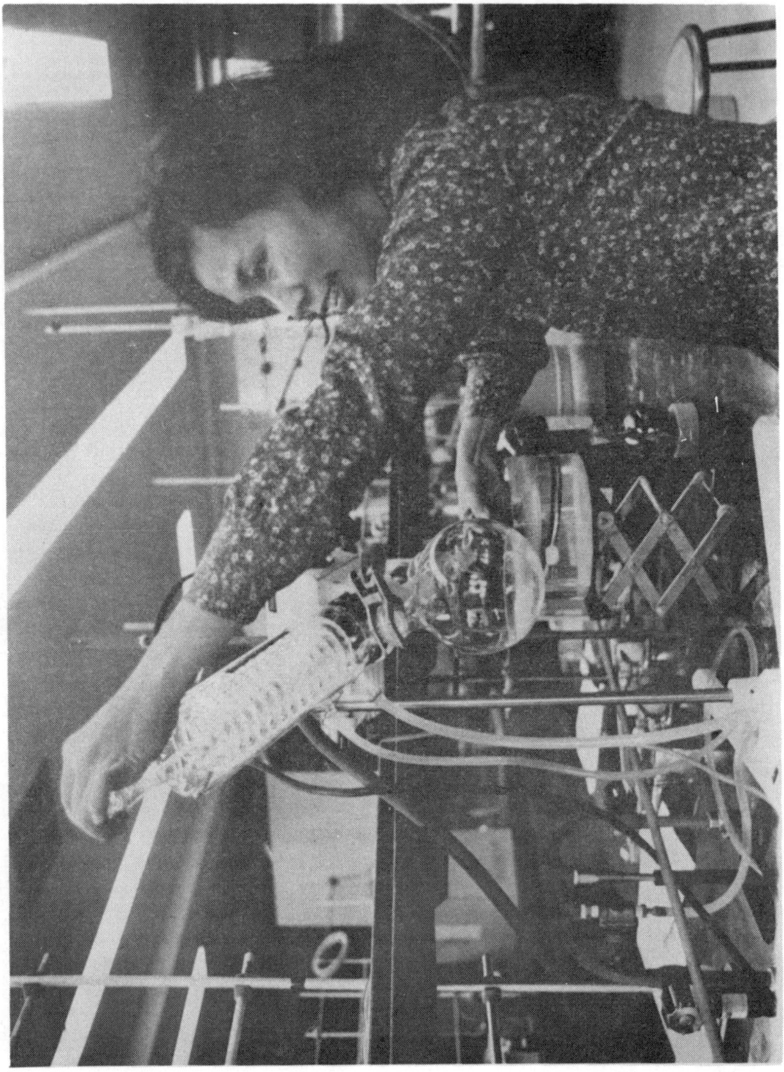

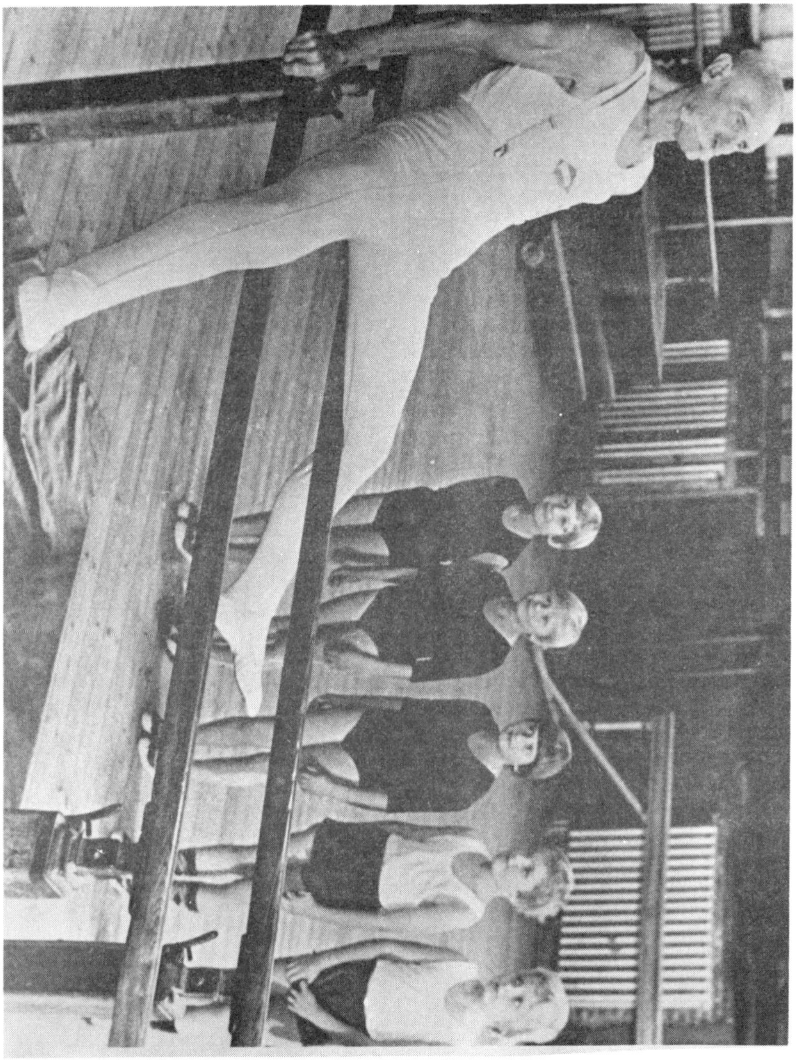

CHAPTER 5

SOME OBSERVATIONS ON LITERACY IN CANADA AND A METHOD TO IMPROVE THE MATCH BETWEEN READING MATERIALS AND READERS

John Cairns and Kristian John Kirkwood

Introduction

In a modern society, Canadians cannot claim their rights as citizens unless they are sufficiently literate to read and understand typical materials which affect them. It is not sufficient for them to learn only from T.V., the radio or conversation, nor to rely on reading in a heritage language like Chinese, German or Italian. Canadians must be adequately literate in an official language to remain citizens possessed of all their rights and opportunities. This ideal has justified huge financial investment for instruction intended to provide basic literacy skills for every citizen.

The notion of basic literacy has become a focal point for discussions on the success of literacy programs, particularly in formal education. It has unfortunately been difficult to determine the degree of success of programs because of the lack of measurement expertise (testing). More importantly, only recently has a valid and reliable criterion level of literacy been established (Bormuth, 1970). Most criticisms of literacy levels in schools and society have been based upon unique criterion levels or have utilized general and somewhat arbitrary criteria. For instance, there are those who define literacy rates as the proportion of adults (those over fifteen years of age) who have more than five years of formal schooling. Still others have utilized standardized school reading tests to estimate adult literacy levels. More innovative researchers have used economic factors such as the volume of paper used by the printing industries or the amount of ink used over a given period of time (Bormuth, 1978). Although there are many factors associated with literacy levels, it appears that no one indicator can definitively evaluate literacy levels.

Lacking consensus about what is an appropriate literacy level and how it should be measured, we need scientific and meaningful methods of literacy evaluation in schools and in the general population. Consequently, the purpose of this chapter is twofold. First, utilizing conventional definitions of literacy (i.e., level of educational attainment) general observations are made about literacy levels of the Canadian population and various subgroups. The second section proposes one specific definition of literacy based on the psycholinguistic model of reading, a linked measurement technique called cloze testing, traditional mechanical readability formulae and certain findings from current research studies in Manitoba and Ontario, especially those of minority official language students in Manitoba.

Literacy in Canada -- An Overview

Literacy has been defined in terms of levels of educational attainment by both UNESCO and most governments. This is recognized to be indirect and only an estimate of literacy levels. However, a substantial body of research corroborates the positive relationship between reading ability and years of formal schooling (Bormuth 1968, Rankin 1959), so it is possible to make some general observations about literacy, using years of schooling as a basic index.

In recent years in advanced industrialized societies, the "illiterate" population has been subdivided into two broad groups: (1) those individuals with less than five years of schooling and (2) those individuals with less than nine years of schooling. Those with more than nine years of schooling are assumed to be literate. These criteria also may be applied to the Canadian population. For example, Table 5.1 summarizes progress for a fifteen year period, showing a real and proportional decline for illiteracy among Canadian adults who have left school.

Table 5.1   Illiteracy Among Canadians Aged 15+, 1961-1976

Year	Total Population 15 years +	Less than Grade 5 #	%	Grades 5 - 8 #	%
1961	11,046,605	1,024,785	9.3	4,141,561	37.5
1971	13,168,020	937,440	7.1	3,961,905	30.1
1976	15,402,030	856,060	5.5	3,520,595	22.8

There are nearly one million adults who have less than grade five education, many of whom probably need basic literacy training. A further three and a half million adults in 1976 had education levels between grades 5 and 8. Most of these will have some basic literacy skills; many will need help with writing, spelling and/or reading skills. This finding has major ramifications for educators who are interested in offering courses to the adult population. If opportunities are available, it is known that adults can learn at any age. People in their seventies have enrolled and continue to enrol in literacy programmes in Canada; more would do so if they knew that programmes were available.

One and a half million Canadians having less than grade 9 schooling are now in the prime period of their adult lives -- 20 to 50 years. The problem is very serious for some ethnic groups (Table 5.2). Slightly more are men than women, and old are less literate than young, all facts to be taken into account by programs.

Table 5.2   Canadian Population 15 Years and Over,
            Not Attending School Full-Time
            by Ethnic Group and Rank
            According to Highest Percentage with
            less than Grade 9, 1971 Census

Ethnic Group	Total 15 Years + n.a.s. f-t	Less than Grade 9 and no other	Percent	Rank
British	5,924,585	1,491,830	25.2	11
French	3,689,690	1,685,585	45.7	3
German	824,725	272,700	33.1	7
Italian	434,930	270,320	62.2	2
Ukrainian	381,380	159,665	41.9	4
Scandinavian	249,870	67,395	27.0	10
Netherlands	237,515	71,740	30.2	8
Polish	207,685	83,600	40.3	5
Jewish	196,345	46,245	23.6	12
Asian Groups	171,150	48,715	28.5	9
Indian & Inuit	148,585	98,935	66.6	1
Other & Unknown	701,585	277,395	39.5	6

Source: Statistics Canada.   Population: The Out-of-School
   Population.   1971 Census of Canada.   Catalogue No. 743,
   Vol. 1, part 2.   Ottawa, 1974.

We can safely say that at least one million adults or 1 in 15 of the Canadian adult population need some kind of basic literacy training: the true need is much greater because of the relativity of the concept, the complexity of modern society, the increasing rate of change, and the fact that nearly half of the adult population have no more than tenth grade educational attainment (Table 5.3, Figure 5.1 and Figure 5.2).

Table 5.3 Population Not Attending School Full-Time by Age Group, Showing Level of Schooling for Canada, 1976 Census

AGE GROUP	Total Population in Age Group	Less than Grade 5	Grades 5-8	Less than Grade 9	Grades 9-10
15-19 yrs.	1,180,870 / 7.7	17,590 / 2.1	122,540 / 3.5	140,130 / 3.2	455,875 / 15.5
20-24 yrs.	1,760,265 / 11.4	20,120 / 2.4	119,170 / 3.4	139,290 / 3.2	292,240 / 10.0
25-29 yrs.	1,912,690 / 12.4	25,880 / 3.0	190,480 / 5.4	216,360 / 4.9	297,965 / 10.2
30-34 yrs.	1,596,640 / 10.4	31,315 / 3.7	240,905 / 6.8	272,220 / 6.2	280,360 / 9.6
35-44 yrs.	2,570,830 / 16.7	91,935 / 10.7	599,735 / 17.0	691,670 / 15.8	518,540 / 17.7
45-54 yrs.	2,459,605 / 16.0	141,805 / 16.6	757,145 / 1.5	898,950 / 20.5	477,685 / 16.3
55-64 yrs.	1,920,765 / 12.5	169,975 / 19.9	670,590 / 19.0	840,565 / 19.2	340,970 / 11.6
65-69 yrs.	722,745 / 4.7	102,035 / 11.9	282,735 / 8.0	384,770 / 8.8	112,335 / 3.8
70 + yrs.	1,277,625 / 8.3	255,405 / 29.8	537,295 / 15.3	798,700 / 18.1	159,220 / 5.4
Total all groups	15,402,030 / 100.1	856,060 / 100.1	3,520,595 / 99.9	4,376,655 / 99.9	2,935,195 / 100.1

Figure 5.1   Population Within Age Groups Not Attending School Full-Time by Level of Schooling

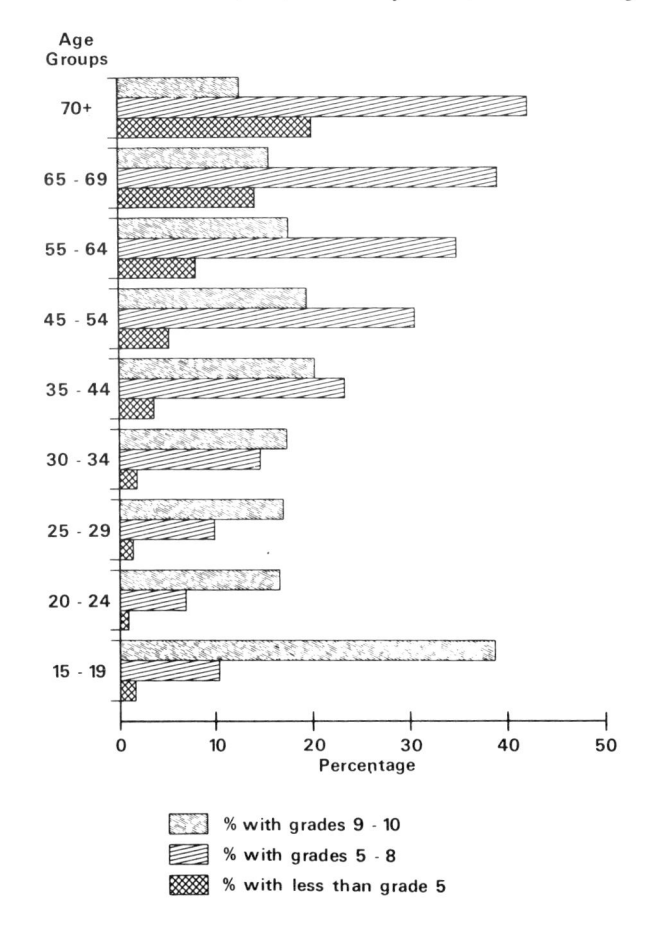

- % with grades 9 - 10
- % with grades 5 - 8
- % with less than grade 5

Source: 1976 Census of Canada Appendix I, Table 15.

- 102 -

Figure 5.2 Canadians Aged 15+, Not Attending School, With Less Than Grade 5 and 10 (Grade 9 in Newfoundland)

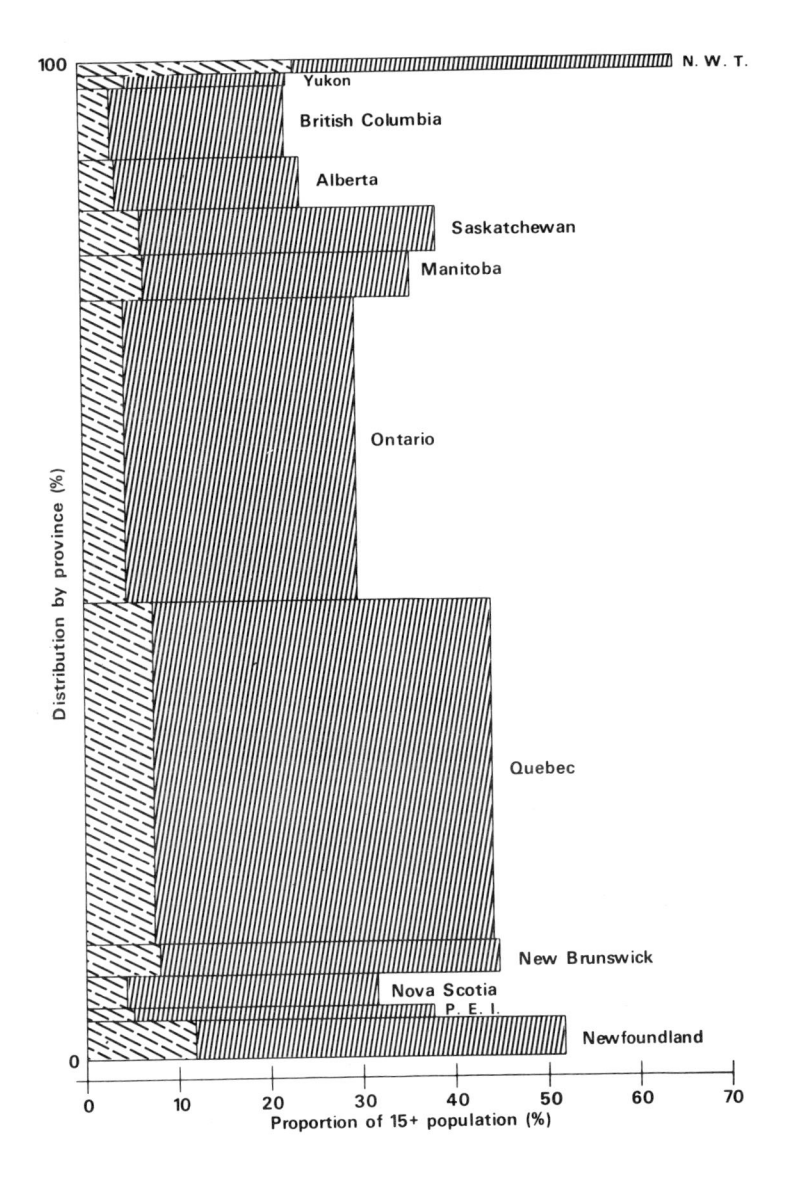

Source: 1976 Census of Canada Appendix I, Table 13.

Table 5.4 presents a summary of the Canadian population 15 years and over, who are not currently attending school full-time, by province, and for Canada as a whole. In addition, levels of education are split into three groups: (1) less than grade five, (2) between grades five and eight, and (3) less than grade nine. Both frequencies and percentages are reported. This table demonstrates some of the inherent problems of defining literacy. For instance, when examining the figures for Canada in the grade five and grade nine groups, we see that the illiteracy rates range from 5.5 percent to 28.4 percent. The figure reported usually represents the researchers' individual bias and the criteria adopted. The data reveal significant discrepancies between the regions. Examining column C (less than grade 9) there appears to be a linear relationship between geographic regions and illiteracy, with 19.1 percent of the British Columbia population with less than grade nine, and Newfoundland reporting 39.8 percent in this category. Another observation from this table is that two thirds of the illiterates of Canada live in Ontario and Quebec.

Table 5.4   Population 15 Years and Over, Not Attending School Full-Time*, Showing Level of Schooling For Canada and the Provinces, 1976 Census

Region	Population 15 years & over	(a) Less than Grade 5**	(b) Grades 5-8	(c) Less than Grade 9	(c) as a % of the Canadian Total
Canada	15,402,025 100	856,060 5.5	3,520,595 22.8	4,376,555 28.4	100.01
Nfd.	338,640 100	40,205 11.9	94,630 27.9	134,835 39.8	3.08
P.E.I.	76,525 100	3,785 4.9	21,185 27.7	24,970 32.6	.57
N.S.	547,595 100	23,560 4.3	125,850 23.0	9,410 27.3	3.41
N.B.	440,820 100	34,555 7.8	127,310 28.9	161,865 36.7	3.70
Quebec	4,191,160 100	312,785 7.5	1,219,725 29.1	1,532,510 36.6	35.02
Ontario	5,550,345 100	246,865 4.4	1,147,070 20.7	1,393,935 25.1	31.85
Manitoba	692,185 100	45,475 6.6	155,820 22.5	201,295 29.1	4.60
Sask.	618,375 100	39,715 6.4	158,630 25.7	198,345 32.1	4.53
Alberta	1,199,855 100	46,150 3.8	194,445 16.2	240,595 20.0	5.50
B.C.	1,708,300 100	56,630 3.3	269,800 15.8	326,430 19.1	7.46
Yukon	14,065 100	700 5.0	1,775 12.6	2,475 17.6	.06
N.W.T.	24,170 100	5,625 23.3	4,355 18.0	9,980 41.3	.23

*Includes 'attending part-time'.

**Includes 'no schooling' and 'kindergarten'.

Source: Statistics Canada. Population: Demographic Characteristics. Level of Schooling by Age Groups. 1976 Census of Canada. Catalogue 92-827. Ottawa, 1978.

Literacy Systems

A large proportion of the information that students are expected to acquire from about grade 4 is transmitted to them through written materials, especially textbooks, reference books, and supplementary reading books. In this connection, the role of the teacher and of educational administrators becomes one of facilitating reading -- through selecting books, assigning reading passages, assisting students in reading -- and evaluating the student's understanding after reading. The success of the information transfer depends to a large extent on whether the students have sufficient linguistic ability to understand the language of the reading material, or conversely, on whether the materials are written at a level of linguistic complexity appropriate to the language ability of the students.

For purposes of this research, the matching of the skill of the reader and the difficulty or accessibility of materials is fundamentally what is meant by "literacy". This definition reflects the research of Bormuth (1968).

The following research analyzed the functional capabilities of the literacy system in Ontario and Manitoba schools. Representative sample students from four Ontario school boards and systematic samples of materials in use in those boards were drawn, and a survey was undertaken using the cloze procedure to compare the skill of the students and the difficulty of the materials (Kirkwood and Wolfe, 1981). Similarly, all French-speaking students in grades four, seven, and ten in Manitoba were surveyed (Kirkwood and Nediger, 1981).

The general conclusion of the research is that there is a substantial mismatch: most of the books in use or available for use are too difficult for most of their potential readers in either language. This will not surprise most classroom teachers (Bormuth, 1977). It is not unreasonable to assume that the same mismatch between readers and reading materials applies to the adult population, but systematic analysis for literacy levels for all ages and segments of Canadian society has not been undertaken to date.

Linking the Literacy Technology to a Reading Model

Psycholinguistics, the combination of cognitive-developmental psychology and linguistics, provides an approach to understanding how students read and how they succeed or fail at extracting information from passages. The primary assumption of the psycholinguistic model is that the search for meaning is the real goal of reading. The process of reading is a cognitive process, in which the reader actively pursues the content or meaning in a passage. This implies that reading is not a simple auditory or visual transformation of print to speech, but rather it is complex, internal information processing, that is, a kind of thinking (Cooper & Petrosky, 1975).

According to psycholinguists, the language represented in a printed text conveys meaning through three kinds of information: the graphophonic information of the marks on the page, the syntactic information, which is implicit in the order of the words of the text, and the semantic information, which derives from the combination of the words, the syntax, and the prior experience and knowledge of the reader. Because syntactic rules link the surface structure of letters on the page with the deep structure of the meaning of what is being read, the process of reading must place great stress on the relationships of words within sentences and of sentences within larger organizations (Cooper & Petrosky, 1975).

Psycholinguistic research is based on the theory that fluent readers read for meaning, not just to identify groups of letters; graphophonic cues, syntactic cues from the text, and considerable prior knowledge of language and content combine to resolve the alternative meanings a sentence or paragraph can have. Beginning readers need more visual information from the printed page, and reading is slower for them because they do not have the stored information and experience which would allow them rapidly to reduce the uncertainty of meaning with a minimum of visual information. Fluent readers need only a minimum of surface structure cues to arrive at the deep syntactic and semantic structure.

A fundamental assumption of research in psycholinguistics is that the brain is directing the eye rather than the eye directing the brain. That is, a reader establishes hypotheses on the basis of partial cues derived from the symbols on the page, makes hypotheses about potential meaning, predicts subsequent parts of the text, verifies hypotheses, and generally takes an active direction in working to an understanding of the meaning of the passage (Cooper & Petrosky, 1976).

This psycholinguistic model for reading leads us to a refined basis for defining and measuring literal comprehension. Generally, evidence is required to substantiate that a reader can and does process the surface and deep levels of information in a text and arrives at a complete conceptualization of the syntactic and semantic structure of the text. Clearly, it will not suffice for a reader to recognize the words in a sentence or paragraph of text; the reader must capture the intricate syntactic connections between words, phrases, and sentences. The obvious implication for adult education is that we must assign appropriate reading materials.

This definition of literal comprehension is operationalized in Bormuth's (1968) original cloze studies, which provide the basic justification for the use of the cloze criterion levels. Bormuth carried out a complete syntactic analysis and breakdown of the language in his passages. He identified each syntactic node and applied a linguistic transformation to the language structure around the node to turn the words into a question. The questions derived in this fashion can be answered by a reader of the passage if the reader has succeeded in processing the syntactic structure of the passage. The set of questions provides a complete examination of the comprehension of the passage. Bormuth's final criterion for information gain is the increase in the number of questions that the student can answer after reading the passage.

The psycholinguistic theory also suggests the kinds of measurements which are appropriate for assessing the comprehension skill of a reader and the reading comprehension difficulty of a text. For readers, it would be ideal to observe the speed and accuracy with which they process the information in a text and to know what array of language transformations they are capable of applying and what level of syntactic and conceptual complexity they are capable of absorbing. For texts, ideal measurement would involve examining the complexities in the complete syntactic structure and determining the amount and difficulty of information processing necessary for deriving the deep structure from the surface content. These are the theoretically ideal measurement procedures, but except for basic calibration studies such as Bormuth's practical applications, require the use of some of the alternative approaches, such as vocabulary knowledge of students and word length in texts. They are statistically correlated with the characteristics of reading ability and readability, and for practical purposes may be substituted for them (Bormuth, 1968; Rankin, 1959). Cloze testing comes closer to the ideal observation because it elicits the information processing activity and allows its progress to be observed.

Cloze Testing for Literal Comprehension

Cloze testing refers to any process in which students are asked to restore original text from text which has been altered or "mutilated" through word deletion. Performance on cloze tests is indexed by how much of the original text the student can recover (Taylor, 1953).

There are various cloze testing procedures involving different deletion rates, use of systematic or random deletion, deletion of certain kinds of words, and so on. There are also various procedures for scoring the tests, including the acceptance of only exact replacements or the acceptance of synonyms for deleted words. The traditional open-ended cloze testing procedure was used in this study. In this procedure, every fifth word is deleted and only the exact replacements are accepted as correct responses. Bormuth (1977) has shown that different deletion procedures produce highly correlated scores. While the mean score levels differ according to the kind of deletion or the kind of acceptable replacements, the ranking of readers and the ranking of passages are relatively unaffected. For the purpose of our studies the cloze procedure was chosen so that this work can be tied to the definitive calibrations of Bormuth.

Traditional cloze procedures operate with mutilated text and require students to replace deleted words exactly. Cloze tests measure literal comprehension because the process of identifying the correct word simulates the process readers go through in reading the passage. Successful substitution for the deleted parts is possible because of the cues in the original language, but the students must use all the syntactic and semantic cues which are visible in the remaining graphic information. In other words, a reader must interact with the particular content and structure of the passage as far as it can be seen in order to consider possible substitutions. The cloze procedure measures the overall concept load and the overall syntactic and semantic processing that must be employed in reading and understanding the passage (Taylor, 1953). Because it depends on the apprehension of the deep syntactic and semantic structure of a passage, it is remarkably free of dependency on the surface differences in the styles of different writers (Walter, 1974). The standard open-ended cloze procedure provides a general measurement of the student's understanding of a passage.

In Bormuth's work, the technique of standard open-ended cloze testing has been shown to have a constant and consistent metric or measurement scale. Bormuth has mapped, over a broad range of both reading materials and student age and reading skills, the relationship between cloze test scores and the criterion outcomes of information gain, time spent in reading, and attitude toward reading. He found that a particular level of cloze response corresponds to a fixed amount of information gain, regardless of whether one deals with fluent readers of difficult passages or with poor readers of easy passages.

The criterion levels suggested by Bormuth have been employed in this study. Bormuth used the judgment of teachers about the relative importance of information gain, attitudes toward reading, and time spent in reading. He fixed a weighting of these three factors to define the general utility of the passage to the student. He then related this general utility to the cloze response level and determined the levels of cloze which optimize utility. He concluded that 35% of cloze response is the minimum for which a passage would be useful to students in terms of basic understanding. At anything less than this, there would be effectively no information gain or else there would be an unwillingness on the part of the student to spend the time necessary to extract information. Bormuth found that 40% or 50% is probably ideal and that 50% and above meant that extracting information would be easier.

Results

In Table 5.5 are presented the overall literacy rates for both the students from Ontario and Manitoba by grade and subject area.

Table 5.5   Overall Literacy Rates by Grade and Subject Area
             for Ontario and Manitoba

Ontario (n=8,701)

Subject	Grade			
	4	7	10	12
Language Arts	28%	38%	57%	64%
Social Studies	15%	37%	53%	---

Manitoba (n=811)

Subject	Grade		
	4	7	10
Language Arts	32%	27%	55%
Social Studies	26%	31%	65%

Clearly, these results indicate that there is a substantial mismatch between books and students for these particular subject areas. Other studies (Bormuth, 1970) have yielded similar results on materials such as newspapers, etc. It is possible to speculate that there are higher illiteracy rates for the public-at-large.

Applications to Educational Practice

In summary, this literacy evaluation research has yielded some immediately interpretable survey results and a set of calibrated measurement procedures which can be used in further practical applications.

It is a practical reality of the educational system in Ontario and Manitoba (and elsewhere) that the reading materials available are of variable terms of language complexity. They are generally too difficult. This is never going to be completely remedied. In any case, the survey and local cloze testing procedures can help teachers make better decisions about selecting and assigning textbooks and about determining the preparatory activities when materials of an ideal level of difficulty are not available. These procedures are as true in adult classes as for primary grades.

As educational programs are developed for technical, vocational, social, cultural or political objectives; it is considered essential that the lessons from this review of literacy be kept in mind. Excellent programs may fail through a failure to communicate properly.

REFERENCES

Adams, Roy J. "Day Release for Literacy Education". Literacy/Alphabetisation, Vol. 5, No. 1, 1980, 3-6.

Adams, R.J., Draper, P.M. and Ducharme, C. Education and Working Canadians. Report of the Commission of Inquiry on Educational Leave and Productivity, June, 1979. Ottawa: Labour Canada, 1979.

Adult Basic Education Consortium. A Five Year Plan for the ABE Consortium. Vancouver: the Consortium and Adult Education, Education Department, University of British Columbia, 1979.

Adult Basic Literacy Curriculum and Resource Guide. Victoria: Province of British Columbia, Ministry of Education, 1980.

Adult Functional Competency: A Summary. Austin: Adult Performance Level Project, University of Texas, 1975.

Bernstein, Judith (ed.). People, Words and Change Literacy Volunteer Handbook. Ottawa: Algonquin College, 1980.

Bormuth, J.R. "Literacy in the Classroom" in Help for the Reading Teacher, William Page (ed.), Urbana, Illinois: National Council of Teachers of English, 1975.

Bormuth, J.R. "Cloze Test Readability: Criterion Reference Scores". Journal of Educational Measurement, Vol. 5, 1968, 189-196.

Bormuth, J.R. Readability Formulas and the Literacy Production Function. University of Chicago, research project funded by U.S. Office of Education and the Reading Research Fund, 1977.

Cairns, John. "Adult Functional Illiteracy in Canada". Convergence, Vol. X, No. 1, 1977.

Callaghan, Mollie. "Fight for Adult Literacy". Quill and

Quire, Vol. 45, No. 7, June, 1979, 13.

Canadian Commission for UNESCO. Adult Education in Canada. Report presented to UNESCO for the Third International Conference on Adult Education, Tokyo, July-August, 1972. Occasional Paper 6. Ottawa: 1972.

Collins, Larry. "The Secret Shame of Illiteracy". Reader's Digest (Canadian), April, 1977, 35-39.

Cook, Wanda Dauksza. Adult Literacy Education in the United States. Newark, Del.: International Reading Association, 1977.

Cooper, C.L. and Petrosky, A.R. "Reading Strategies and Teaching Implications for Secondary Schools from the Psycholinguistic Model of the Reading Process". The High School Journal, 59(2), November, 1975, 91-102.

Cooper, C.L. and Petrosky, A.R. "A Psycholinguistic View of the Fluent Reading Process". The Journal of Reading, 20(3), December, 1976, 184-207.

Dickinson, Gary. "Canada's Undereducated Adults". Learning, Vol. 2, No. 1, 1978, 9-11.

Draper, James A. and Clark, Ralph J. Adult Basic and Literacy Education: Teaching and Support Programs within Selected Colleges and Universities in Canada. Toronto: Department of Adult Education, The Ontario Institute for Studies in Education, 1980.

Final Report: International Symposium for Literacy. Persepolis, Iran, 3-8 September, 1975. Paris: International Coordination Secretariat for Literacy, 1975.

Goodman, K.S. "Psycholinguistic Universals in the Reading Process". In F. Smith (ed.), Psycholinguistics and Reading. Toronto: Holt, Rinehart and Winston, 1973, 21-27.

Goody, Jack (ed.). *Literacy in Traditional Societies*. Cambridge: University Press, 1968.

Hansen, L.H. and Hesse, K.D. *A criterion-referenced assessment of reading literacy using the cloze procedure*. Illinois: American Educational Research Association, 1974 (ERIC Document Reproduction Service No. ED 090 314).

Hate, M.A. and Kane, R.B. "The Cloze Procedure as a Measure of Mathematical English". *The Journal for Research in Mathematics Education*, 6(2), March, 1975, 121-127.

International Council for Adult Education. *The World of Literacy: Policy Research, and Action*. Ottawa: International Development Research Centre, 1979.

Kidd, J.R. *Functional Literacy and International Development: A Study of Canadian Capability to Assist with the World Campaign to Eradicate Illiteracy*. Ottawa: Canadian National Commission for UNESCO, 1967.

Kirkwood, K.J. and Nediger, W.G. *Matching Students and Reading Materials*. Winnipeg: Department of Education, 1981.

"Literacy and Development", *The NFE Exchange*, Issue No. 17, 1980.

McLeish, John. "Knowledge and Revolution: The Student Movement in Tsarist Society (1856-1881)". *The Alberta Journal of Educational Research*, Vol. XXIII, No. 2, June, 1977, 151-163.

McLeish, John. "The Russian Sunday Schools -- An Experiment in Voluntarism". *The Alberta Journal of Educational Research*, Vol. XX, No. 1, March, 1974, 75-95.

McLeish, John. "The Soviet Conquest of Illiteracy". *The Alberta Journal of Educational Research*, Vol. XVIII, No. 4, December, 1972, 307-326.

Smith, Frank. *Comprehension and learning*. Toronto: Holt,

Rinehart and Winston, 1973.

Smith, Frank. Psycholinguistics and reading. Toronto: Holt, Rinehart and Winston, 1973.

Taylor, Insup. Introduction to Psycholinguistics. Montreal, Toronto: Holt, Rinehart and Winston, 1976.

Taylor, Wilson L. "Cloze Procedure: A New Tool for Measuring Readability". Journalism Quarterly, 30, Fall, 1973, 415-433.

The Experimental World Literacy Programme: A Critical Assessment. Paris: The UNESCO Press, UNDP, 1976.

Thelen, J.N. "Using the Cloze Test with Science Textbooks". Science and children, 12(3), 1974, 26-27.

Thomas, Audrey M. "Adult Literacy -- A Challenge for the '80s". VIEWS, The Adult Education Journal of the Saskatchewan Association for Lifelong Learning, 1980, 29-37.

Thomas, Audrey M. "Adult Literacy -- New Challenges". Learning, Vol. 2, No. 3, Spring, 1979, 10.

Thomas, Audrey M. "Illiteracy in Canada". Canadian Library Journal, Vol. 37, No. 4, August, 1980, 215-218.

Thomas, Audrey M. "The Movement for Canadian Literacy". The Reader, Vol. 1, No. 2, 1979, 5-11.

CHAPTER 6

VALUES OF CANADIAN ADULTS
AND
TECHNICAL AND VOCATIONAL EDUCATION

D. Stuart Conger
and
M. Catherine Casserly

In July, 1978, psychologists at the International Congress of Applied Psychology in Munich questionned aspects of work values and the salience of work in people's lives. They decided to develop instruments which could measure these constructs and then to compare the results internationally. This report on the Work Importance Study presents results from the Canadian first trial use instruments.

The rewards sought from work have been conceptualized as 'work values' and this term refers to the desire for particular kinds of satisfaction in work. The relative importance attached to work as opposed to various other activities which an individual may engage in has been termed 'work salience' (Super, 1978). This term subsumes many precisely defined phenomena previously considered under such headings as 'job involvement', 'career commitment', 'central life interests' and, in some senses, 'alienation from work'.

The Work Importance Study involves research teams from 15

countries, each conducting coordinated parallel studies. The common objective has been to establish conceptually adequate models of work values and work salience, and to operationalize them in the form of readily administered measures appropriate for use in each of the participating countries. The national projects have been launched by interested psychologists, invited by Professor Donald Super of Columbia University and the National Institute for Careers Education and Counselling. Some participants are university faculty members who have obtained government or private funding, others are staff members of institutes or ministries interested in the problems (Super, 1981).

Each team initially reviewed the national literature on research in this area. In Canada, a great deal of work had never been published in journals but was available as government publications, theses, and research papers from a variety of sources such as universities. This material was compiled using the following four hypotheses:

1. There are social class and other subcultural differences in work and work values.

2. There are sex differences in work salience and work values scores and profiles.

3. Work increases in importance, in comparison with other life roles, as the entry into employment approaches.

4. Adjustment to work is related to work salience, work values and the extent to which those values have been realized in the job obtained (Casserly and Cote, 1980).

Social Class and Subcultural Differences

Forcese (1980) summarized the socio-economic situation in Canada as a nation of economic extremes. There are regional, rural, urban and ethnic disparities. Generally, the Atlantic region seems least affluent, and major metropolitan areas in Ontario, Alberta and British Columbia seem the most prosperous.

A Canadian characteristic is the small town existing around a single industry, such as a mine, paper mill or railroad. Unlike established towns in places like the Maritimes and Quebec, these towns are peopled by those who are young, married, of rural background, and from ethnically diverse origins (Jackson and Poushinsky, 1971). Unlike most Canadians, these residents tend to be very mobile geographically. They predominate in many of the primary resource towns across the country.

In terms of differences in values between linguistic groups, most previous research has compared the workers of Quebec with those in the rest of Canada. On virtually all dimensions of work-related opinion and attitude, when differences exist, all French-Canadian employees, but especially those at the rank and file level, feel more positively than do their English-Canadian counterparts (Nightingale, 1975). Such differences appear to arise from two factors. The first is that English-Canadians have higher expectations and are therefore less likely to achieve satisfaction. Secondly, Francophones are more likely to experience communication difficulties and tend not to welcome changes in job location. Further, Francophones attached greater importance to extrinsic interpersonal and organizational factors such as associates, altruism, prestige and security (McCarry et al., 1977).

Research on cultural differences and the work salience between whites and natives shows that Native Canadians face many barriers to employment. The average unemployment rate on reserves in 1978 was 48% (Employment and Immigration Canada, 1979). Natives face five major problems in the world of work. First, the majority live in rural environments, often hundreds of miles from cities where non-skilled jobs are available and relocation is perceived as a frightening experience. Second, Natives often experience cultural alienation working in the white world. Third, Natives lack training for typical jobs in an industrialized economy. Fourth, many adult Indians, Inuit, and Metis are not fluent in either English or French. Fifth, many Natives fear that employment in a white society will result in cultural genocide.

Sex Differences

The greater proportion of a woman's adult life is now spent working outside the home (Burstein et al., 1975). Fewer women than men identified working with the provision of basic economic needs. Women were more oriented to the family in terms of achieving personal goals, and, accordingly, expressed less attachment to their jobs than did men. Their different reasons for working did appear to influence the importance women attached to various aspects of work, and to make them more selective of types of employment. For example, women felt amenities associated with work to be more important than did men so they were more willing to accept lower salaries. Women were also less concerned with the availability of promotional opportunities and the chance to get ahead. Greater importance was placed by female respondents on the supervisory aspect of their jobs.

Entry to Work Force

Our third hypothesis dealt with the increasing value placed on the worker role as time of entry into employment approaches. There are two major groups to be considered, youths with no experience in the labour market and re-entry people who are usually older women. To date, the research has focused on the young. The Canadian Work Values Study (Burstein et al., 1975) pointed to the greater importance young people placed on peer groups and friendly co-workers. Young workers were more optimistic about the possibility of getting employment. (Recent difficulties faced by youths seeking work may well have changed this, at least temporarily.) Both young and older Canadians viewed work as being the primary means of obtaining success. The differences between age groups lay not in the importance they placed on work, but on the relative emphasis they placed on friends and family; younger persons more often considered friends to be the key to self-fulfillment and a means of attaining personal goals, while older persons more frequently felt that family provided these rewards. The vast majority of young people desired 'career' jobs. For older groups, most felt either that they already were in such jobs or they had abandoned their aspirations for careers. Although young, career-oriented workers were more likely to change jobs than were their older counterparts, they were also less selective in the kind of work they would accept.

In describing their ideal job, young workers emphasized the importance of supportive resources, good personal relations, and having pleasant and convenient work. Salary was least important to them. The 25 to 34 year olds, on the other hand, de-emphasized personal relations and personal working conditions and placed greater importance than other age groups did on challenging, well-paid jobs. Although it is difficult to establish a trend, over-all it appeared the importance of intrinsic job factors increases with age as compared to extrinsic factors.

Adjustment to Work

Our fourth hypothesis stated that adjustment to work is related to work salience, work values, and the extent to which those values have been realized on the job. The Job Satisfaction Survey (Burstein et al., 1975) indicated that nearly 90% of Canadian workers obtained some job satisfaction. This majority reported fewer job changes and periods of unemployment, less desire to leave current jobs, and a greater sense of long-term commitment to a job. They were far less likely to consider that they could get a better job and were more likely to describe their jobs as being 'careers'. In describing ideal jobs, they wanted work to be interesting, to have enough information and authority to do the job, and to have the opportunity to develop special abilities. Of lesser importance were job security, promotional considerations, pay, work hours, and fringe benefits. When aspects of jobs were ranked according to the satisfaction they provided in current employment, having enough authority and information, friendliness of co-workers and supervisors, interesting tasks, and seeing the results of one's work were more important than job security, work hours, quality of supervision, pay, fringe benefits and promotional opportunities.

The International Instrument

From the literature available in Canada we developed a list of values considered to be important. The international teams met and chose 23 values to be used in the first stage of the research (Figure 1). In subsequent meetings, items developed to measure each of these values were agreed, then translated into the national language or languages. In Canada, versions in both English and French were prepared and distributed for field trial to members of the Canadian team. This sample of convenience included universities, colleges, secondary schools, counselling centres and employers.

In Canada, English and French versions of the <u>General Values Scale</u> and the <u>Work Values Scale</u> each consisted of 5 items for each of 22 values. The major difference between the general and work values scales was that one focused on work or job and the other did not. There was some controversy on whether or not the general values of most persons differ from their specific values. A large number of subjects completed both forms in order that this concept could be studied. In subsequent research, the scales were reduced to a smaller number of items and combined into a single measure.

Figure 6.1 **The Values Selected for the International Study: Stage One**

1. ABILITY UTILIZATION

    Freedom to use and to develop one's talents and skills, and to find outlets for one's interests in the things one does.

2. ACHIEVEMENT

    Doing something well, the feeling one gets from doing or having done something well.

3. ADVANCEMENT

   Promotion, upwards mobility in terms of progression in one's career, increases in opportunity to learn, and to increase the use of abilities, to do more interesting things, to have a better standard of living, to live in a better environment, and to have a better income.

4. AESTHETICS

   Adding to and enjoying the beauty of processes, products and surroundings, both natural and man-made.

5. ALTRUISM

   Helping others and being concerned for their welfare.

6. ASSOCIATES AND SOCIAL INTERACTION

   Valuing pleasant, friendly contact with the people with whom one associates in work, in the home, in leisure, including attending to and talking with people, being part of a social organization.

7. AUTHORITY

   Influence over others which requires others to follow a point of view or policy, or which leads others to believe that they should accept it. It can be wielded through position, power, expertise, charisma or seniority.

8. AUTONOMY

   Making one's decisions and carrying out plans as one sees fit; independence of action within one's own sphere.

9. CREATIVITY

   Developing or making something original, which may not be something unique, never before produced or made, but is original for the person concerned. The product may be an object, writing, painting or other art work, an idea, a new method, or an organizational method.

10. ECONOMIC REWARDS

    Economic rewards such as salary, bonuses, benefits, income from investments; the personal possessions and real property that income makes possible.

11. ECONOMIC SECURITY

    Stability of income, assurance of being able to live in the desired way without threat to one's economic or social well-being.

12. ENVIRONMENT

    The physical surroundings, whether at school, university, work, at home, in leisure activities or in the community.

13. INTELLECTUAL STIMULATION

    Opportunity to learn and to think independently, to solve problems.

14. LIFE STYLE

    The preferred way of life, which is defined in a number of different ways such as conventional, conservative, liberal, radical, intellectual, artistic, materialistic, or traditional. These examples have in common the freedom to live as one wishes, according to one's own standards and values.

15. PARTICIPATION IN ORGANIZATIONAL DECISION MAKING

    Taking part in any aspect of making decisions that effect the life or functioning of a group, whether at work, in the family or in the community. Includes the identification of problems, the actual decision making, and the implementation of the decisions.

16. PRESTIGE

    Social, economic or occupational status which arouses respect, esteem, and admiration; the recognition of achievements or of personal qualities.

17. RESPONSIBILITY

    The power and knowledge for decision making; being accountable for the consequences of actions taken.

18. RISK-TAKING AND SAFETY

    The excitement of physical danger, financial gain or loss, and other risks incurred in projects proposed or undertaken; or obversely, freedom from such dangers and risks and from having to cope with the unforeseen and the unknown.

19. SPIRITUAL VALUES

    Communing with an entity that is greater than oneself, observing religious or ethical principles; serving God, society, or mankind.

20. SUPERVISORY RELATION

    Support and structure, fairness, a pleasant relationship with those in responsible positions such as supervisors and other key figures at work, in the home, and in the community.

21. VARIETY

Change and diversity in what one does, whether of tasks, processes and methods, the rhythm of activity, location, or people with whom one associates.

22. CULTURAL IDENTITY

Freedom to conduct oneself, in public and private life, according to the mores of one's primary group or groups (e.g., the family, ethnic origin, and religious membership); opportunity to identify with such personally important groups and to behave as they do.

23. PHYSICAL ACTIVITY (not used in Canada)

General Demographic Data

There were 2,664 completed forms in the overall study; 1,350 General Values Scales (Form A) and 1,314 Work-Related Values Scales (Form B). Sixty-seven percent were in English and the remaining 32.3% in French.

The initial respondents were 48.3% female and 51.7% male. Fifty-eight percent were less than 19 years old, 30.7% between 20 and 40, and 11.3% were over 40 years of age.

Most were English or French (41.2% English and 42.5% French, language first learned; 47.0% English and 45.8% French, language used at home; and 47.9% English, 30.9% French, and 9.9% both, language used at work).

Since 64.1% of the respondents are full-time students, it is not surprising that approximately 57.0% of the total have no work experience. On the other hand, 17.3% had one to 10 years and 20.2% over 10 years experience. In terms of workplace, 72.7% of the respondents work indoors and 88.5% in an urban environment.

Many respondents were unable to estimate their personal or family income. Of those reporting personal income, 20.5%

earned less than $4,999, 6% between $5,000 and $11,999, 21.8% between $12,000 and $26,000, and 8.5% over $26,000. There were 27.4% who reported their family income to be $26,000 or more. The majority of respondents are in the lower-middle and middle socio-economic class.

Over 87% of subjects were born in Canada. While 87.2% of the overall sample were non-native (non Indian/Inuit), a significant number of natives were among the English respondents.

Relocation data for the past five years was examined. The returns indicate 38.3% movement within and 10.9% outside the respective provinces for the participants in the Work Importance Study. This indicates a fairly high rate of mobility for the subject population.

Overall, the sample was fairly representative of Canadians, as a whole.

Section B

General Results, Anglophone and Francophone Subjects

Anglophones, on the general scale, rated as Important (in order): Economic Security, Life Style, Ability Utilization, Advancement, Achievement, Responsibility, Autonomy, Supervisory Relations, Associates and Social Interaction, Intellectual Stimulation, Participation in Organizational Decision Making, and Prestige. On the work-related scale, Economic Security, Ability Utilization, Achievement, Supervisory Relations, Economic Rewards, and Intellectual Stimulation are given Important ratings.

Moderately important ratings on the general scale are given for the values: Altruism, Environment, Spiritual Values, Variety, Creativity, and Aesthetics. On the job scale, Advancement, Environment, Participation in Organizational Decision Making, Altruism, Prestige, Responsibility, Spiritual Values, Associates and Social

Interactions, Autonomy, Creativity, Life Style, and Variety are moderately important.

English respondents gave low importance ratings on the general scale for Economic Rewards, Authority, Risk-Taking and Safety, and Cultural Identity. The work-related values considered of low importance include: Aesthetics, Authority, Risk-Taking and Safety, and Cultural Identity.

This profile contrasts with Francophones who rated important the value Altruism on the general scale. The French respondents rated Intellectual Stimulation and Prestige moderately important whereas Anglophones rated them important.

On the work-related scale, Francophones consider important the values: Altruism, Associates and Social Interactions, Environment, and Participation in Organizational Decision Making. Moderately important ratings are given to: Aesthetics, Cultural Identity, and Risk-Taking and Safety.

Individual Items from the Work Importance Study

In the scoring 1 is most important and 5 is least important.

Ability utilization deals with the opportunity to use skills at which one is especially adept. This appears to be a very important value for all respondents. As a group, they want to use their own particular skills, both in a general way, and in a specific sense where they can maximize the utilization of these skills in the workplace. French respondents (x = 1.5) consider this value to be slightly more important than English subjects (x = 1.7).

Achievement emphasizes accomplishment on the job rather than progress in a career. This value is important to all respondents in both a general (x = 1.7) and specific sense (x = 1.7). Both English (x = 2.2) and French (x = 2.2) rate doing things that will result in lasting changes as less important.

Advancement relates to the concept of upward mobility. In general, advancement is considered important by all respondents. In the work-related scale, it is also important but several items affect the score upwards. The items concerning competitive situations (e.g., 'work where getting ahead is considered important') are rated of less importance.

Aesthetics deals with the opportunity to engage in work which allows one to appreciate beauty. In both a general and work-related way, this value is considered to be of moderate importance. On the general scale, however, it is rated more important by French respondents ($x = 2.0$). The French subjects rate making things beautiful as important ($x = 1.8$); the English rate it unimportant ($x = 2.7$).

Altruism emphasizes helping others. On both the general ($x = 1.8$) and work-related ($x = 1.8$) scales the French respondents rate this item as very important. Anglophones score their responses in the moderately important range on both scales ($x = 2.0$, $x = 2.1$).

Associates and Social Interaction relates to working with supportive associates and having opportunities for good social interaction. The results suggest it is an important value when considered in a general way. (English $x = 1.9$, French $x = 1.7$). While on the job, it is of less importance to be afforded such opportunities but still important to be with friendly people (English $x = 1.8$, French $x = 1.9$).

Authority represents a willingness to assume responsibility for other people. For all respondents, any time the questions relate to this value, there are negative ratings, i.e., the issue is considered unimportant.

Autonomy can be thought of as responsibility for oneself without undue interference from others. Generally, this was considered as an important value for both Anglophones ($x = 1.8$) and Francophones ($x = 1.9$). In the job situation, however, respondents were willing to take direction and have others assume responsibility, especially in the operational aspects of the workplace dealing with issues like hours of work and work schedules.

Creativity is rated of only moderate importance. This finding is borne out with respect to general and work-specific areas.

Cultural Identity emphasizes the freedom to conduct oneself according to the mores of one's primary group. In terms of relating to other ethnic groups, both English and French appear to be equally open-minded. What is of importance to them as a group is the opportunity and freedom to work in one's own language. Similarly, it is important to both Anglophones (x = 1.9) and Francophones (x = 1.7) to be able to work where they are free of discrimination. Francophones (x = 1.8), however, feel it is more important to be accepted at work as a member of their race or ethnic group than do English respondents (x = 2.4).

Economic Rewards concern the acquisition of goods for services rendered. In the general scale it is rated as unimportant by most of the respondents except for good housing, which is rated very important by both English (x = 1.8) and French (x = 1.8) respondents. The average rating for this scale is greatly influenced by the negative response given to several items (i.e., 'Be able to live well without working' and 'Be able to retire early'). Indications are that all respondents want to work and continue to do so for a long time. Job-rewards are rated quite important. When considered by itself, earning enough to live well is considered very important (English x = 1.6, French x = 1.4).

Economic Security refers to the assurance of a stable income. This value is of great importance to all respondents. Having a secure future receives the most consistent rating of importance of any single item on the general scale (English x = 1.4, French x = 1.4).

Environment concerns one's physical surroundings. In a general way this is a moderately important value for both English (x = 2.0) and French (x = 2.0) respondents. Francophones place emphasis on the setting in which they do things (x = 1.4). In a job-specific way, the French and English rate the environment as being similar in importance.

Intellectual Stimulation deals with the opportunity to learn new things and solve problems. Both in a general and in a job-specific way, all subjects want the chance to deal with new ideas and learn new skills.

Life Style relates to the freedom to live as one wishes, according to one's own standards and values. On the general scale it is of great importance for all respondents. But although Canadians want to shape the decisions that affect their own lives, on the job, it is of less importance. Both the English and the French are more willing to accept the organization's rules, expectations, and obligations so long as they do not affect their own philosophies. On the job-specific scale, English respondents (x = 2.3) rate this value slightly less important than Francophones (x = 2.1). Anglophones appear to be a little more willing to accept organizational constraints while at work.

Participation in Organizational Decision Making is a value related to shaping the direction of one's own life (i.e., 'Share in decisions that will affect me') which is important to both Anglophones (x = 1.9) and Francophones (x = 1.9). Similarly, being kept informed about everything that could possible affect one's life is important. However, on the job, issues like 'being able to shape the policies of the employer' are considered less significant (English x = 2.2, French x = 2.4).

Prestige reflects socio-economic status, respect, esteem, admiration, and recognition. English respondents (x = 1.9) rate it as being slightly more important in the global aspects of their lives than do the French subjects (x = 2.0). Francophones gave this value a moderate rating on general and work-related scales. On the job-specific scale, Francophone respondents (x = 1.5) rate 'Prestige because of their work' as far more important than do Anglophones (x = 2.2).

Responsibility emphasizes accountability for one's own actions and that of others. The general scale deals with the self, and both English and French respondents consider this value to be very important. In the job-specific scale there is a mixture of items reflecting responsibility both for oneself and for others. Items dealing with responsibility for others are rated unimportant; being one's own boss is likewise unimportant (English $x = 2.5$, French $x = 2.7$). However, it is important that one's work be taken into account in assigning credit or blame.

Risk-Taking and Safety relates to the element of danger either through loss of face or physical injury. All respondents strongly reject granting importance to placing themselves in physical danger. Even in the areas of taking chances when the only cost might be loss of face, respondents are still quite unwilling, as a group, to enter into such a challenging situation.

Spiritual Values relate to the concept of communing with entities greater than oneself. On both the general and work-related scales the values have moderate importance for both English and French respondents. There is, however, some emphasis placed on being able to live by one's own moral or ethical standards. All respondents, especially the French ($x = 1.5$), rated strongly that one should work in ways that take their fellow workers into consideration.

Supervisory Relations focus on how the individual relates to or is treated by those in superior positions. All respondents desired placement where they could have fair treatment. Canadians appear to want to know what is expected of them and want to be measured fairly against that standard.

Variety deals with the desire for change and diversity in one's life and work. Both in a general and in a job-specific way, this appears to be moderately important for all respondents. Francophones ($x = 1.9$) rate being able to move around while working somewhat more important than English subjects ($x = 2.3$).

Applications for Vocational Education

It is obvious from this research that technical and vocational education must be compatible with the important values of Canadians, especially related to economic security, ability utilization, achievement and advancement within a job as well as the quality of supervisory relations. The technical and vocational skills that are relevant to the values of Canadians may, therefore, be summed up as: (1) job skills, (2) personal financial management skills, (3) opportunity utilization skills and (4) skills of working with seniors in one's occupation in order to maintain a good relationship.

Given the above results, it is quite obvious that there is a definite need for continuing technical and vocational education and training that increases one's ability to do the present job, shows one how to exploit new opportunities to use one's existing talents, and to deal with bosses. The immediacy and specificity implied by these values was supported by the work of Allen Tough (1982) which showed that each year almost everyone chooses to spend at least 7 hours learning something useful, and that, on average, does so eight times a year. However, relatively seldom was the learning project extended over several months and only 1% of the projects were part of a formal education program. Tough found that the most frequent type of learning project was one related to one's job or occupation. The fact that his findings are comparable with the values of Canadians as well as with measures of how Canadians spend their time (Harvey, Elliott and MacDonald, 1983) suggests that this pattern will continue.

Given this situation plus the increasing proportion of the population who are free to choose the type and duration of their training, if any, it would appear that credit or even half-credit courses may be too long for most people who seek training and that credit for units of continuing credit may be more appropriate if significantly more adults are to take part in formal training. A second requirement deriving from the values of Canadians is that they want defensive human relation skills or social survival skills. Based upon our research, it can be concluded that the importance of technical or vocational educaton to the values of Canadians is to help them to survive. There is no dream.

Our second conclusion is that given the values of Canadians and their strong need for economic security, it must be recognized that decisions on particular learning projects will be made with some concern for anticipated economic conditions and particularly forecasted occupational supply and demand. At the present time in Canada, there are a number of very important changes occurring which affect the labour market including the aging of the population so that the average Canadian is now 29.6 years old, the aging of industries in central and eastern Canada and the strong demand for highly qualified people in business and technology-oriented occupations.

The situation, therefore, presents some very special issues for technical and vocational training of adults because it appears that many workers will require a significant amount of training but will not want to endanger their present jobs to obtain this training. And one cannot expect that it will necessarily be available through on-the-job training because employers may not have the skill and financial resources to carry out the training.

One answer to the problem of the effective delivery of intensive training at convenient times will be the delivery of training to homes by means of computer-assisted learning packages that can operate on home computer systems or, eventually, on Telidon-compatible terminals in the home.

Such training programs can probably be learned in the time that it would normally take a person to travel to and from classes. Furthermore, they can effectively teach all cognitive material and have only laboratory components of the training which need to be conducted centrally.

In the next few years, the field of vocational and technical education must change drastically in order to respond to the changing values and lifestyles in Canada.

REFERENCES

Baba, V., and Janal M. "Company Satisfaction, Company Commitment, and Work Involvement", *Industrial Relations*, 31, (13), 1976.

Bujold, Charles. "Signification du travail et valeurs de travail: revue de la litterature canadienne de langue francaise", *L'orientation professionelle*, 16, (i), 1980, pp. 5-47.

Burstein, M., Tienhaara, N., Hewson, P. and Warrander, B. *Canadian Work Values - Findings of a Work Ethic Survey and a Job Satisfaction Survey* (Ottawa: Employment and Immigration Canada, 1980).

Casserly, M.C. and Cote, L. *The Work Importance Study in the Canadian Context* (Ottawa: Employment and Immigration Canada, 1980).

Campbell, A., Converse, P.E. and Rogers, W.L. *The Quality of American Life* (New York: Russel Sage, 1976).

Dumazedier, J. *Sociology of Leisure* (Amersdam: Elsevier, 1974).

Employment and Immigration Canada. *The Development of an Employment Policy for Indian, Inuit and Metis People* (Ottawa: Author, 1979).

Employment and Immigration Canada. *Labour Market Development in 1980's* (Ottawa: Author, 1981).

Forcese, Dennis. *The Canadian Class Structure* (Toronto: McGraw-Hill Ryerson Ltd., 1980).

Harvey, A.S., Elliott, D.H. and MacDonald, W.S. *The Work of Canadians*, Vol. 3 of Explorations in Time Use (Ottawa: Canada Employment and Immigration Commission and Communications Canada, 1983).

Jackson, J.W., and Poushinsky, N. Migration to Northern Mining Communities: Structural and Social-Psychological Dimensions (Winnipeg: Centre for Settlement Studies, University of Manitoba, 1971).

Knasel, E.G., Super, D.E. and Kidd, J.M. Work Salience and Work Values: Their Dimensions, Assessment and Significance (Cambridge, England: National Institute for Careers Education and Counselling, 1981).

McCarrey, M.W., Edwards, S. and Jones, R. "The Influence of ethno-linguisticgroup membership, sex and position level on motivational orientation of Canadian Anglophone and Francophone Employees", Canadian Journal of Behavioural Sciences, 9 (3), 1977, pp. 274-282.

Nightingale, D.V. "The French-Canadian Worker Shows Up Well in the Study", The Canadian Personnel and Industrial Relations Journal, 22 (5), 1975, pp. 28-30.

Roberts, K. Leisure (London: Longmans, 1970).

Roberts, K. Contemporary Society and the Growth of Leisure (London: Longmans, 1978).

Super, D.E. Career Education and the Meaning of Work (Washington: U.S. Government Printing Office, 1975).

Super, D.E. "The Babble that is Babel", Journal of Career Education, 5, 1978, pp. 156-171.

Super, D.E. "A Life-Span, Life-Space Approach to Career Development", Journal of Vocational Behaviour, 16, 1980, pp. 282-298.

Tough, A. Intentional Changes (Chicago: Follett Publishing Co., 1982).

Vroom, V.H. Work and Motivation (New York: Wiley, 1964).

CHAPTER 7

LIFE-LONG EDUCATION AND PERSONAL FULFILMENT: AN EXPLORATION OF IMPLICATIONS FOR LATER YEARS

David Radcliffe

This chapter examines the general evidence that death is increasingly associated with old age, that more individuals survive to attain a full "normal" life span, and that the proportion of elderly persons in the population is steadily rising. This makes it possible to speculate about a phase of life referred to as "the Third Age",(1) although social perception and understanding provides no precedent for this phenomenon (Laslett 1979). The Third Age is therefore both a descriptive and a creative term, and it will be necessary to explore some of the meanings accruing to the concept before examining the creative role of education, for, in, and

---

(1) There is already debate about terminology, with partisan support for elders, elderly, older persons, persons of later years, seniors, etc. The Third Age is derived from the French Troisieme age, distinguishing it from First Age/Formative Years, Second Age/Middle Years generally associated with employment, and Fourth Age/terminal dependency. The term seems to be gaining international currency.

about the Third Age. The role of education will also depend upon an exploration of the idea of personal fulfillment, and its variations according to individual life experiences, social and cultural situations.

Perhaps the main determinant of a Third Age is the more familiar concept of retirement, but whereas retirement has generally a negative connotation even when qualified as "active retirement" (retirement from an active working life) proponents of the concept of a Third Age intend it to be understood as a new and positive phase of life. Nevertheless in our current society there is a relationship between Third Age and exclusion from the workforce. This connection is particularly important in a society which tends to "equate human worth with earnings" and thus "renders the elderly valueless to society" (Kreps 1979).

When we consider education and the later years from age 55 onwards, which currently include pre-retirement preparation and the transition to retirement, we note that there is nothing magic about age 60, or 65 as a mark of transition in the life course, except as a social convention for which Bismarck is mainly to blame. Achenbaum (1978) and Phillipson (1979) show that the concept of retirement permitted the elderly to be given very cavalier treatment: their "value" has fluctuated with the economy.

In many ways the presumed incapacity of the elderly can be compared to the presumed incapacity of youth; the former no longer able to cope with the demands of a changing workplace, and the latter as yet ill-prepared. This materialistic evaluation is doubly unjust to older persons. It assumes that while there are justifications for investment in the formative education of the young, in the First Age, the elderly have exhausted their contribution to society. It also assumes that it is possible to identify a convenient chronological age at which human obsolescence sets in, a belief challenged by proponents of the plasticity model of adult cognitive development such as Neugarten, Schaie and Labouvie-Vief (Allman 1981). The Third Age is a social and cultural concept which cannot be chronologically defined except in terms of ephemeral social conventions. Sometimes these conventions give rise to marked anomalies. One useful definition of old-age for the demographer might be the point at which average life expectancy becomes less than ten years (Abrams 1981). In Canada this would currently make it 70 for men and 75 for women, a striking difference and reversal of present retirement conventions of 65 for men and 60 for women. The Third Age is predominantly a female group. Not only do women predominate in numbers but they are less likely to be shouldered into obscurity by retirement because they usually maintain their traditional sex related household activities.

The Third Age provides social and personal recognition of a new period of life during which employment in order to support oneself and one's spouse will cease or be phased out, yet expects a continuing high level of personal and household autonomy, backed by physical and mental independence. This transitional phase of life eventually gives way at various ages to the "old" old. Third Age thinking recognizes that this period may extend forwards with trends to earlier retirement conditioned by economic forces, although this tendency may be moderated by flexible retirement, or smooth phasing out of employment at least for individual cases. There is concern that as this phase of life becomes more normal, the Third Age should be valued, respected and enjoyed like earlier years, and that adequate social provision should be made to secure this. Given adequate recognition, preparation and support, it will be possible to minimize the material dependency of the Third Age, and to identify and encourage a contribution that will counter criticisms based on a dependency ratio which stresses only the transfer of income between generations (Myles 1982).

The danger of adopting Third Age as a convenient category is that it may become glibly endowed with a set of characteristics and stereotypes which negate the reality of human diversity. John Nicholson (1980) discounts the theory of predictable stages and crises in life and rejects the suggestion "that the difficulties we encounter at different times in life are the inevitable consequences of a universal development cycle which affects everybody, irrespective of the events which occur in a particular person's life". Many

of the French Universites du Troisieme Age reflect similar
thinking with formulations such as "inter-ages", "tous ages"
or "pour tous". In brief, then, the main determining factor
in the predicament of the Third Age is not aging per se, it
is the linking of age with social integration.

Personal fulfillment is very obviously a subjective
matter, though it is influenced by social conditioning. What
we would value for our later years will be modified by what
we have been led to expect. One of the problems to be faced
by education for the later years is the dead-weight of
out-moded mythology about physical and intellectual capacity,
attitudes which for many older persons become self-fulfilling
prophecies. "In our value system, we believe that the
elderly are non-productive, unattractive, useless, garrulous,
old-fashioned.... When we are young, we absorb those notions
on a subconscious level and when we reach that age period we
have a built-in system of self depreciaton, causing the
elderly themselves to shun the very notion of being old"
(Kreps 1975). It is this kind of attitude that lent support
to the validity of "disengagement theory" as the pattern for
optimum aging (Cumming and Henry, 1961) as the pattern for
optimum aging. Neugarten (1970) identified a range of
differing personality types (Figure 7.1):

Figure 7.1   Personality Types and Aging

I	Integrated	A	Re-organizers
		B	Focused
		C	Disengaged
II	Armour-Defended	D	Holding-on
		E	Constricted
III	Passive-Dependent	F	Succorance-Seeking
		G	Apathetic
IV	Unintegrated	H	Disorganized

Sidney Jones (1976) has attempted to relate these types to learning needs. His conclusions suggest a range of possibilities, from non-intervention through basic needs and supportive reassurance to enrichment and recirculation for some. In these, the positive cope most successfully, re-organizers plunge into a round of new activities, the focused have more limited goals such as house-improvements or some defined social activity, while the disengaged are the quintessential contented rocking-chair types. For the first two categories enrichment programs or job re-orientation courses of the kind that are already frequently available would be suitable, although in many cases they know how to get what they need, for example from public libraries. For the rocking-chair type no intervention is needed.

The armour-defended are threatened by aging, and respond by holding-on to the patterns of middle-age, resisting any alternatives or offers of assistance. Here the problem is greater, since although they feel anxious because of social pressure to retire, they develop physical problems that impair their performance, they are likely also to reject the idea of needing educational help, or the possibility of educational intervention. Jones suggests structured alternatives such as voluntary work for those who are holding-on. For the constricted (i.e., those who are "pre-occupied with losses and deficits and deal with these threats by conserving their energies and closing themselves off from experience") the situation is superficially similar to the disengaged, though it is motivated by anxiety rather than by acceptance. The potential for the role of the media, T.V. and radio, to reach out to this particular group could be investigated. But the problems of this category of persons are peculiarly caused by social conditioning, and one solution lies in general education for all to come to a better understanding of aging. The armour-defended are fighting against learnt deprecation and forced incapacity not by refuting, but by admitting the social stereotype while denying it for themselves.

Jones deals with the apathetic and the disorganized together. Although they both reflect varying levels of inability to cope and basic dependency; in the case of the disorganized, dependency may be concealed by original or bizarre behaviour. He identifies here a "therapeutic and possibly evangelistic social task for education". However the "succorance-seeking" are likely to be quite a large proportion of the retired population and they present the clearest demands for educational services. This category of persons is not apathetic, and is conscious of new opportunities (often the opportunity to take up interests that had to be missed in the past) but is "able to perceive the threat to ... well-being and morale which the inactive, purposeless and pointless pursuits of an empty retirement could bring [and feels] helpless in the face of such emptiness". Jones sees here the potential for greatly expanded educational support leading both to personal fulfillment and the maintenance of the independence and autonomy which self-respect requires. Without such support, there is the danger of depression becoming progressively severe, and consequently increased dependency.

Clearly these categories of adjustment to aging are not static. Changing conditions and crises, health and disease, bereavement, financial security or anxiety, can result in progression towards or regression from the Eriksonian concept of "ego integrity" (1976). Similarly, Margaret Mead (1960) proposed that education be phased according to individual needs: Phase I, those who are young or vulnerable or slow growing and need strong supporting individual relationships; Phase II, those who are ready to learn in groups, standardized information or behaviour, the products of higher civilization; Phase III, those who are growing so unevenly that they require protection in some sectors of life if learning, growth, and achievement are to be possible in other sectors of life ("this phase includes ... all adolescents, whether adolescence ends at fifteen or sixteen, as it does for some girls, or extends to old age, as it does for some gifted and one-sided artists, scientists and statesmen"); Phase IV, those who are mature, "whose need for special protection from the community is minimal". Mead's schema stresses that these phases do not represent a chronological progression, and may recur throughout the life course. It is not difficult to see that Neugarten's classification could be equally valid for what she has called an "age irrelevant" society, except perhaps that the defences of the armour-defended would no longer be necessary.

We should begin to transcend the stereotypes of chronological age in order to recognize how such stereotypes are socially conditioned and therefore amenable to educational revision. But for those persons now in and approaching the later years, certain beliefs about aging hold sway. Of particular importance to education, there are unjustified assumptions about declining intellectual ability and of the difficulty of "returning" to educational activity. These deny the value of a lifetime of experiential growth and relegate learning to narrowly defined patterns of formal education. Initially we need remedial programs to rescue both education and its clients from this misunderstanding.

A longer lifespan for a significant proportion of the population justifies educational provision both as a human right and as a social necessity in order to promote self-reliance and autonomy (Kidd/Ray 1983). James Birren (1978) refers to the "drop-out aged" who "have been overpowered and have not developed immunity to the many facets of living, as opposed to the accomplished aged who behaviorally, socially, and physiologically have developed immunity and are perhaps stronger as a result of longer years". We need an understanding of normal old aging which allows for individual variation, but provides an understanding of basic competencies which would in turn assist the formulation of educational needs to assure such competencies, and thus helps to prevent "drop out". Although pre-retirement education programs already address this problem, there is a dearth of studies to evaluate their effectiveness.

Birren's comment suggests "accomplished aging" to be a development process which takes place over a period of years -- over the whole life course. The "immunity" of which he speaks results from life-long understanding of and acceptance of aging as growing, and this in turn implies a radical change from an education system which places excessive stress on the early years as the formative period of life. To treat the later years as a special phase with peculiar needs makes sense only in the situation in which the middle years have been neglected, and the later years denied altogether.

Finally, we should take note of some caution. The education system is immensely powerful, but with declines in the birth-rate and falling enrolment in the traditional years of education, it is under pressure. There is a danger of educational colonialism, with middle and old age as new frontiers. In particular the later years are at risk since formal education has always justified exclusion from the "world of work". Education for social acceptance is not the same thing as education for personal fulfillment, and while recognizing the prophylactic role of education in postponing the loss of self-reliance, we should also recognize its custodial tendencies. As with youth, education for older persons could be justified because they are becoming a liability without it. It could become a device for social control, justified because their members give the elderly political power, to ensure they exercise this power "properly". Ideally it should be justified because the fundamental condition of life is change, and no one is better qualified to understand change and mediate that understanding to society through the medium of education than the old who have experienced it longest. The task of education is to liberate that understanding, and thus validate the contribution of the later years.

- 1459 -

The migration projections indicate large movements out of Ontario and Quebec, into Alberta and British Columbia, and smaller streams heading for Saskatchewan, Nova Scotia, and across to Manitoba. However it should be noted that the even impacts of migration from migration. The substantial differences among the sizes of alternative projections for Ontario reflect the wide range of expected rates of regional growth, industrial growth, changing industry-employment ratios, and the ability of employment to keep abreast of future regional population growth. Future growth of Recent Research (Dept. of Adult Education, University of Nottingham, 1981). growth and prosperity probably will be greatest in those provinces where the most innovative approaches have been adopted. Overwhelmingly that is in the industry and commerce of the 21st Century. Changes are likely to the adaptability of existing industry. Heavy industries like spinning and weaving in the southern Ontario (Basic Books and Newfoundland, as well as iron and steel in Ontario and Quebec have low industry-employment ratios because they are already extensively mechanized. Modern technologies, especially the new Daedalus, Spring 1970 like cars, combines, and rail and subway equipment, as well as to industries like textiles and boot and shoe making with its Learning and Employment Patterns in Ontario and Preparation for Retirement: New Approaches (Dept. of Johnson Foundation, 1976) investment in the traditionally high employment industries like textiles and boots and shoes is expected. Robert and Douglas Ray in International Adult Education of the emerging Human Rights, much Canadian advanced country, continued Human Rights in Canadian Education (Kendall/Hunt, 1983) spinning, weaving and finishing textiles, are all in view. Kreps, Juanita. "Human Values, Economic Values and the Elderly" in New Technologies in Death and the Completion of Being (University Press, 1979) even more important. Future forestry in British Columbia, for Kreps and Juanita. "The Economy and the Aged" in the Handbook of Livestock demand for fisheries, and Handbook of Aging and the Social Sciences need to see the mid-sized wood construction industry which is the biggest employer in the province. Quebec and New Brunswick probably will better pulp and paper in English family and the aged world Chena Society" in McKee, J. Meng T., ed., Aging, Death and the Completion of Being (University study on the Pennsylvania, Depends upon 1970 world markets, particularly those of the United States.

CHAPTER 8

AN ASSESSMENT OF EXISTING AND EMERGING THIRD AGE CONTINUING EDUCATION PROGRAMS FOR SOCIAL AWARENESS AND POLITICAL PARTICIPATION

C.G. Gifford

Context

Although the values held by persons constitute one major determinant of social awareness and political participation, other major components are the global political imperatives of the time and the resources and knowledge available to the learner/actors in the situation. This chapter is an assessment of the global political imperatives which currently confront our values, with special emphasis on the role of mature citizens.

Projections of population, prosperity and the roles of educational institutions will all be profoundly affected by provincial, national, and especially international political decisions over the coming years. The values of our citizens are not fixed; they will be modified by events.

Although political decisions are crucial to the nature of our future, we don't make decisions _as a nation_. Persons at the helms of such institutions as EXXON, the Royal Bank, the CPR, the Chase Manhattan Bank, and of national, provincial and foreign governments, make the decisions. In the nation, province, or community, the citizens' role is primarily to respond periodically to the useful but very crude and ambiguous choices which are offered at elections. These choices are offered. Citizens rarely initiate them, and to have any creative part in them is a laborious and often a socially risky proposition.

Can we make political projections parallel to the demographic and economic projections which have been provided in earlier chapters? I suggest that neither population nor economic studies can have much realism unless we also attempt to assess some of the forces at work and the political choices which thrust themselves before our attention.

Who in 1924 "projected" the depression of the 1930s? Who in 1910 projected the slaughter of a generation of British, French, German and Russian youth between 1914 and 1918? Who in 1940 projected that the number of communist countries would increase from a single super power to two super powers and at least fifteen smaller communist states? What is on the horizon of a similar order? These events did not just happen; they resulted from conscious choices by certain persons. And what are the implications for adult learning in order to broaden participation in Canada's choices, to promote or to resist certain possibilities?

There is a very substantial literature, both fictional and analytical, which deals with possible futures, for example Nevil Shute's "On the Beach," Doris Lessing's "The Four Gated City," Hugh MacLennan's "Voices in Time," Rachel Carson's "Silent Spring," Paul Erdmann's "The Last Days of America," Roberto Vacca's "The Coming Dark Age," Buckminster Fuller's "Utopia or Oblivion," The Club of Rome's various scenarios, Robert Heilbroner's "An Enquiry into the Human Prospect," and Isaac Azimov's "A Choice of Castastrophes." All of these argue that present patterns of intranational, international, and extra-national behavior will lead to destruction, and some of them suggest personal or collective behaviour that might avert it.

Canada has been one of the few major portions of spaceship earth to escape the full force of most previous disasters. Of the four hundred inter- and intra-national armed conflicts since World War II, Canadians have been combattants only once. The thirty years since then is the longest period of 'peace' in Canada's history. Even as a Colony, Canada did not experience the usual extensive violent racial and military repression; and our losses in the two World Wars were slight in comparison to those of France, Russia, Britain, and Germany. No foreign war has been fought on Canadian soil for 160 years; we have escaped the prolonged and wracking civil wars of China, Vietnam, El Salvador, Ethiopia, Nigeria, Lebanon, Northern Ireland, etc. We have <u>suffered</u> far less than people of other parts of the globe. Perhaps we grew politically blase, fattened by the economic and social sweetness achieved since 1940, anaesthetized to the painful realities which have been common elsewhere. It may take more effort for Canadians to identify and examine political changes which threaten us with political and economic convulsions.

The Ultimate Challenge

We face drastic global political choices. Continuation of the present industrial and commercial patterns and the present military and trade policies will lead to societal collapse through exhaustion of resources, pollution, famine and the struggle within and among nations to increase their share of a diminishing pie.

The various alternatives to current patterns all ultimately involve a slow-down of industrial growth, the transfer of resources from war (defence) to life enhancing uses, and the promotion of class, racial, and national equity in the distribution of the globe's wealth. These alternatives ultimately require an ethos of equity and toleration (or better, appreciation) of differences among cultural, religious and political groups. Although such changes require an end to much of the material excesses and waste which now are part of the lifestyles of middle and upper classes in 'Northern' nations, they would allow civilization to survive.

The possibility of ending civilization through nuclear war looms. One former diplomat, now in his 90's, recently argued:

In our short time on Earth, we have a choice about the kind of world we leave behind. With nuclear weapons in our custody, our generation carries a heavy obligation. There will be no historian to record one day that we failed in our watch (Harriman, 1981).

Lord Louis Montbatten condemned nuclear weapons shortly before he was murdered; two admirals and eleven generals recently retired from senior positions within the North Atlantic Treaty Organization, called for the removal of all nuclear weapons from the arsenals of all European Countries (Globe and Mail, Nov. 8, 1981). Andrei Sakharov, Robert Openheimer, Hyman B. Rickover and Robert McNamara are among the most prominent names condemning the idea of nuclear war. Scientists, politicians, military and diplomatic leaders are among those condemning the arms race. Grey heads of citizens in many occupations are conspicuous in photographs of public demonstrations for peace.

Present political and transnational corporation establishments often lead us further into the danger. The military tunnel vision which led the German, British and French leaders into World War I remains dominant in U.S. and Russian military and political establishments, and in most despotisms striving to keep their disgruntled citizens in check.

If we cannot expect a change of direction from the military industrial establishment of its own volition, can it come from the citizens of Canada and other democratic countries? For example, can those few nations which at present control and consume 80% of the world's resources accept the necessary changes in their citizens' lifestyle and require their governments to do likewise? Of course it is possible, but what are the educational implications? Much must be learned about the reasons for current global and national problems, about realistic alternatives, and about methods of exerting democratic political power.

The political issues which must be addressed are global in scope: we cannot project a Canadian future which is somehow immune from the convulsions around us. The politics of metropolitan urbanization, of home care rather than institutionalizaton for the frail elderly, of Quebec Separatism, and other specific community or immediately Canadian issues must be put into the global context which is their real setting.

Most Canadians are distracted by what the students in the student revolt in France in 1968 called "Le spectacle", which means that they adhere to the values which extra-national corporations and the governments of the "great" powers so avidly promote. They are also beset by a sense of political powerlessness.

But most serious is that they cannot match the resources available to private profit-oriented interest groups to bombard us through television, the printed word, and radio; propaganda which is consumerist, escapist and sensational (Halberstam 1979, 214-215). Such freedom to advertise and to anaesthetise is not an essential democratic right. In France, Britain, Germany and Holland, advertising is limited to brief and specific periods which will not interrupt the flow of programming, and considerable resources are devoted to public interest issues. Canadians must repossess the airwaves, so that along with being entertained, we can learn about the drastic political changes which are all around us, and can release ourselves from the "business as usual" psychology which stems from our relatively placid history.

Media stimulation to "think the unthinkable" has occurred in limited areas, such as the recognition of China or open discussion of sex. Within the next 10 years can we take the far more difficult step of first debating and then beginning to dismantle the war system, for example?

Such considerations imply that social awareness and political participation should be priority items on the agenda of life-long education. By what means and in what contexts are matters of urgent importance.

Life-long Education Initiatives of Retired Persons

The social awareness and political participation of retired persons is important not only because their numbers are significant - currently, approximately one voter out of seven in Canada is 65 years of age or over and not only because some are active in political parties. About the time of retirement, persons have the time and the life experience to study and reflect on our political situation, and they are freer of the functional constraints which employed people experience - the risks to jobs, to promotion, etc. - and therefore have less to lose by thoughtful and committed political action than people at earlier life-cycle stages. United, informed action on the part of even a very small proportion of this segment of the population could be an important political force.

What then are the values of Canadians over fifty-five years of age, with respect to participation in experiences aimed at enhancing their social awareness and their political participation? Eighty-five percent of Canadians over 65, and 86% of those aged 36-65 vote in federal elections (Mishler 1979, 103). Does the great involvement of seniors in voting and in active political participation lead to greater interest in enhancement of knowledge and skill in these areas? Can one generalize about persons over fifty-five years of age, or do cohort effects lead to substantial differences among segments of this population? (E.g., people now in their seventies were too young for World War I, tended to gain employment in the twenties which continued into the thirties, and were too old for World War II, whereas people now in their sixties were too young to be employed in the twenties and then faced unemployment during the thirties and mobilization during World War II. Is there a difference attributable to this difference in cohort experience?)

Parents wish to leave an inheritance to their children

and grandchildren. This has financial meaning but does it now have some political content? Are any seniors motivated by a concern for the kind of community, country, and world which their generation is passing on (or failing to pass on) to their descendants? One response may answer these questions: I want to be an ancestor instead of part of the last generation.

The idea has been widely debated by very ordinary old persons at the club and federation level. Resolutions related to such issues have been passed by the National Pensioners' and Senior Citizens' organizations, reflecting a general concern for social justice and peace, rather than anxiety about their personal descendents.

Although some seniors' leaders complain about their members' passivity, preoccupation with social activities and resistance to intellectual engagement, many seniors are organizing to create vital learning experiences for themselves. One model for this is the "Learning and Living in Retirement" (LLIR) organization, founded by a group of retirees in Toronto in 1973, as a result of a one-day workshop at the Ontario Institute for Studies in Education with support from York University. LLIR has a 20-person board chosen by a membership of 800. Janet McPhee (one of the founders and for three years its president) stated that the members "want to be brought up to date about the world of politics, the world of science, Canada's place in the world, etc." The topics, instructional format and overall program arrangements (including associated social activities), are all organized by a program committee in consultation with the total membership and with the aid of a program consultant. The topics chosen have included current economic issues, science and society, man in society, political science and government.

LLIR spawned "Third Age Learning Associates (TALA), a free information centre", with an office at Glendon College of York University. It is an "independent, volunteer group (which) came into being because of a perceived need – the need of seniors in Ontario for the intellectual and social stimulus of learning _together_" (their emphasis) (TALA 1980).

TALA seeks to address primarily the needs and concerns of seniors who had "an unsatisfied hunger for intellectual sustenance." Enhancing political awareness was stated as the first objective of LLIR.

A smaller, but nonetheless significant, educational effort of seniors is "Development Education in Action" (DEA), which links the "struggle (which) is required if older people are to regain their independence and become creative again" with concerns for "social issues in Canada and the Third World." While the group engages in self education, it applies the results in action through producing slide-tape montages which the members then show, with discussion, to schools and community groups (Talnews 1981).

Each province has a federation of senior citizens groups, and in at least six provinces there is an additional province-wide senior citizens' organization. In British Columbia, there are two federations, which in 1981 joined with about 15 other retiree organizations to form the B.C. Committee of Senior Citizens' Organizations (COSCO), linking more than three thousand senior citizens clubs and centres. There is also the National Pensioners and Senior Citizens' Federation, a loose federation of provincial and local organizations.

Thus far, with one exception, there are few ongoing linkages between these organizations and universities or other post secondary education programs. University instructors occasionally ask the organizations' leaders to speak to classes but the associations rarely ask universities for research or instructional assistance. Why this reluctance? A spokesman for the British Columbia organizations (a man in his seventies with an MA in sociology) expressed considerable scepticism about both the professionals in the field of gerontology and the likely utility of university courses and continuing education offerings for seniors. His view was that most university people tend to be "out to lunch" so far as seniors are concerned, are patronizing towards them, and make the egregious mistake of planning _for_ seniors rather than responding to the seniors' own planning. Whether these views result from or conflict with experience in courses for seniors put on by Simon Fraser University (which later were transferred to local senior centres with the facilitation of the Simon Fraser Continuing Education staff), is not known.

The exception mentioned above was the Continuing Education Department of the Université de Montréal, which had taken a social animation role in relation to the development of the Association Québecoise pour la Défense des Droits des Retraites et Préretraites (AQDR). Even here, after a four year developmental period, a very active and politically experienced seventy-seven year old leader for AQDR said that the personnel of the University of Montreal Continuing Education Department tend to direct rather than to facilitate the activities of the AQDR, a tendency which he tactfully deplored. The AQDR appears to be exclusively political in its goals and behaviour.

All of these provincial organizations and the national organization attempt political influence. In some cases their potential political significance is clearly recognized by both federal and provincial governments: there are special annual cabinet or cabinet committee meetings with the executive committee of the organization, Premiers and Cabinet Ministers attend their annual conferences and other significant meetings, ministries respond promptly to enquiries or proposals from these organizations. When the Social Credit Government in British Columbia tried to apply financial restraint to certain benefits for senior citizens, it stepped into a hornet's nest of well publicized protests by the seniors' organizations, so it continued to charge only 75% of the usual premium for public auto insurance for senior citizens.

A few of these organizations prepare sophisticated, well-researched briefs with respect to such issues as housing, pension policy, and in the case of the AQDR, wider issues such as variations in longevity for residents of the slums of Montreal and the suburbs, and the implications thereof.

Six of the provincial organizations (Seniors Action Now

in B.C. and Saskatchewan, Canadian Pensioners Concerned in Alberta, Ontario, and Nova Scotia, and the AQDR in Quebec) have primarily political objectives. These six groups involve no more than ten thousand members. Their effectiveness stems largely from committee studies: they rely little upon organized learning experiences.

Most senior citizens are organized into their own clubs and centres, which although members of the provincial federations, at the local level are primarily social and leisure oriented. Six hundred thousand Canadian seniors participate in such clubs and centres. During municipal, provincial, or federal elections, they invite candidates to speak and may seek to influence policy on issues of vital concern to the members. Films and reports on travel experiences, card games, dancing, and refreshments are popular programme items. The Fédération de l'Age d'Or du Québec, which has nine hundred and fifty constituent groups and one hundred and fifty-thousand dues-paying members, provides some leadership training for club executive officers. Although accepting the desirability of such training, in other provinces the organizations have rarely sought help from educational institutions or included more extensive educational activities within their program planning. The annual provincial and national conventions, with the resolutions emanating from some of the clubs, are the principal form of political participation and learning. Some federations (e.g., The Manitoba Society of Seniors), have ongoing "issues committees."

It is only a matter of time before these organizations realize their own potential both for generating more extensive educational programs with their members, and for more systematic and determined political engagement. Their house organs all pay close attention to policies concerning rent, pensions, retirement, health and other areas of vital interest to senior citizens. Their national organization takes positions on broad matters such as energy policy, Canada's relationship to the third world, the death penalty, wage and price controls and interest rates. Canadian organizations have yet to develop very sophisticated organizations like the American Association of Retired

Persons, The National Council of Senior Citizens and the Gray Panthers.

The Senior Citizens Centres across the country include a growing educational programming component. These centres not only have their own educational activities, but they may also provide the locale for post-secondary extension courses offered to seniors but open to others. Some of the courses could be defined as social/political awareness offerings.

In summary, there are currently four organizational forms of senior citizen-originated educational programs: (1) the seniors' educational organizations (such as LLIR, TALA, and DEA) which are concentrated in Ontario, and have a primarily political self-education focus; (2) study of political issues and processes by the political action groups in six provinces (Canadian Pensioners' Concerned, Seniors Action Now, and AQDR) as part of their preparation for fulfilment of their policy-influence objectives; (3) the rather embryonic educational activities of the clubs which make up the provincial federations and the bulk of National Pensioners and Senior Citizens Organization; and (4) the senior centres which include political and other educational offerings in their programs. In the latter two categories, latent political interests and needs have only begun to be touched. Only the first two categories appear to have drawn on the expertise of professional adult educators or the other resources of post-secondary institutions.

Learning Opportunities Offered by Post Secondary Education and Other Community Institutions

One can think of life-long education as taking place in formal settings - the credit and continuing education programs of universities and community colleges, and the continuing education programs of provincial departments of education - usually in courses, seminars and workshops. Learning also occurs in the informal networks in which a person grows to adulthood and lives his or her life - the family, the peer group, and the informal interaction of the work group and community groups of all kinds.

Many Canadian universities allow seniors to take regular credit classes by admitting them without fees if they have reached sixty or sixty-five years of age. Some actively promote this; others merely list it in calendars. A few are reviewing the policy in the light of financial pressures. Although senior enrolments appear to be small, they may well be the vanguard of an increasing group. Statistics are incomplete but one has the impression that courses on aging and on cultural topics are more popular than are courses in sociology, political science, social work or any of the natural sciences.

Continuing education increasingly provides personal interest courses for seniors or for populations which include seniors. Such courses are sometimes offered in senior centres rather than on campus. Most of them deal with local history rather than social history, provide self-development rather than community development experiences, or deal with creative activities in the arts and crafts, dancing, etc., rather than in the political sphere. The LLIR experience suggests that there may be a considerable untapped market for non-credit courses on public issues and on the citizen role.

The University of Regina operates a Seniors' Educational Centre in the downtown area, at which 576 people enrolled in non-credit studies in 1980 (Saskatchwan Senior 1980).

Elderhostel, which began in the Atlantic Region and a few Ontario and Quebec universities this past summer, included some social awareness courses such as Acadian history, Managing New Brunswick's Forests, The Media and Society, Energy and You, Mistress/Mother/Maid/or Person, and the Quest for World Peace, but had a greater number of courses on cultural topics such as The Joy of Music, Family History, The War of 1812 in the Niagara Peninsula, for example. No Elderhostel courses dealt directly with political participation. Of course, these topics have been determined by curriculum committees or professors of continuing education faculties and departments, sometimes in consultation with seniors, and sometimes not. The British Columbia universities have an indigenous version of the

Elderhostel concept.

Some universities (e.g., Western Ontario, Toronto) have senior alumni programs, often open to their spouses and friends. While these consist largely of service and public relations functions, they include educational offerings planned with and for the Alumni. Topics have included a small number of social/political awareness topics.

Continuing Education divisions of provincial departments of education sometimes provide courses for seniors, including experimental projects in British Columbia, and assistance in the organization of seniors' clubs in Nova Scotia.

It should be noted that there are no absolute dividing lines distinguishing literacy education, education for self-fulfillment, vocational and technical education, and education for social and political awareness and participation. All of the first three become accessible because of political decisions about allocations of resources, and all of them in turn have an impact (whether this is articulated or not) on the students' awareness of and participation in family, community, and state decision making.

Any institution which wishes to serve older Canadians in the educational sphere will need to abandon standard classroom formats and to work in close consultation with the seniors in determining both the content and the delivery method for whatever learning experiences are to be provided. Indeed, it may be that the most successful programs will be ones where these organizations have taken the initiative.

As the educational level of persons over 55 rises, so the interest and ability to use organized learning experiences will rise, but these seniors will likely wish to do a great deal of the organizing themselves. The 15 leaders of seniors political organizations interviewed are heavily involved in political participation, but they vary in the scope of their concerns. They are of middle class and professional backgrounds (teachers, clergy, business, trades union) and all appear to be in secure financial

circumstances. Except for the AQDR, I was able to find
little evidence of any conscious goal of these organizations
to speak for or to engage low income elderly in their
political activities. Only three of these leaders showed
active concern about the global political context.

The informal or instrumental sector is a myriad of
'non-educational' organizations which have an educational
component: religious, cultural, and social settings like in
churches, museums, libraries, community centres; popular
movements and organizations such as the Canadian Legion, The
Women's Institutes, Service Clubs, Labour Unions, Farmers'
and Fishermens' Unions, Cooperatives, Senior Citizens'
Federations; major functional components of our political
economy, such as Cooperatives, government departments, the
military, and in fact all employing organizations; community
organizations with avowed social awareness goals such as
Right to Life, human rights, OXFAM, Amnesty International,
Help the Aged, United Way; environmental groups, etc.;
cultural/educational producers, including radio and
television systems, the National Film Board and other film
producers; social awareness cultural groups or individuals
such as theatre groups, some popular singers, producers of
print; and, finally, political parties.

Among these are a few (the Canadian Legion, the Orange
Lodges, the Imperial Order of the Daughters of the Empire,
perhaps the Women's Institute and some lay church
associations) which are aging as organizations, i.e., the
original basis of membership has little value to recent
generations and so the average age of members has gradually
moved to the senior citizen category.

Most of these groups have a direct or indirect social
awareness and political participation component, either as a
by-product of some service function or as an element in a
training program. For example, a National Safety League
veteran provides training in all aspects of motorcycle
operation, including legal aspects and the need for informed
legislation. Many kinds of community adult learning
activities which are part of the fabric of our society seem
to be technical in nature, or the "mere" pursuit of hobbies

(philately, weekend railroading, whitewater canoeing, gourmet cooking - the list is endless), but all have some potential for political involvement, and may stimulate some form of individual or collective lobbying.

Political learning was investigated for three non-partisan but politics-related organizations - the militia, Nova Scotia's environmental action organization, and OXFAM, a third-world service organization. Regionally employed officials of each organization were asked the nature of social awareness and political participation learning they provide, and whether there is any specific focus on seniors as part of this.

The militia training is essentially technical in nature except for officers. Political learning becomes intensive when one reaches senior ranks, in late 30's or 40's, and parti,cipates in the one year program of the National Defence College. Links with universities exist, through strategic studies institutes and through military studies chairs at five Canadian universities, funded by the Department of National Defence, which could play a role in continuing education programs.

Persons who leave the military can remain on the supplementary list until age 65. Since retirement from regular service in some trades is 55, this means that a person may remain on the supplementary list for 10 years after the age normally considered the minimum for "senior citizen" status. My informants stated that a large number of retired officers continue supplementary list roles. However, except for the National Defence College program, learning provisions within the military are largely technical. Any political aspects of service are taken for granted as reflected in the functions assigned to the military by the cabinet.

The Ecology Action Centre presents a marked contrast so far as resources are concerned. In the militia, even the part-time volunteers are paid. In the environmental movement, apparently even the employed staff risk not being paid, occasionally, since funding is a constant struggle.

Yet the commitment to the cause is high, and massive volumes of work are done by highly qualified but lowly paid employees, and by unpaid volunteers. Formal educational activities consist of a public lecture series at the Nova Scotia Museum, radio interviews, and a newsletter for subscribers. However, the main educational functions of the Centre are as a resource for schools; the conduct of demonstration projects, e.g., recycling newspapers; maintaining an extensive reference library; and giving consultation when requested by community groups (e.g., regarding uranium exploration) for both technical information and for information about what can be done politically. The Centre has also fostered non-credit practical courses on such topics as solar energy and organic gardening, which have been very popular. There are many requests to speak at public meetings and to cooperate with other groups, especially church groups. Many of the volunteers who man its office and library are young but seniors are also involved.

Oxfam, though its function is very different from that of the Ecology Action Centre, operates on the same scale - an office with a resource library, a small employed staff and substantial unpaid volunteer staff. Its chief function is to raise money to assist self-help projects in developing countries, and to "promote an awareness (in Canadians) of the problems these overseas communities face, and possible solutions to those problems. Addressing the causes of underdevelopment is just as important as immediate relief from the results of underdevelopment."

Oxfam does a great deal of direct-mail fund-raising, and is careful that every piece of fund-raising literature has educational content. It sponsors cross-Canada tours of Canadian staff who have worked in the developing world, visitors from problem locations (e.g., recently a trade unionist from El Salvador was financed to speak to trade unions, church groups, and public meetings about the conflict in that country from the perspective of peasants and factory workers). Such visits are used by the media; Oxfam also has produced films, slide shows, and a book.

While organizations like the above are not

age-segregated, retirees are likely to play special roles and engage in associated learning, because they have more time than younger groups, and an accumulation of skill and wisdom related to the subject area, and because they are not constrained by career-related ambitions or mores.

Conclusions

1. Because we face unprecedented global political imperatives; including the fact that political and economic establishments which dominate current Canadian experience are incapable of responding to these imperatives realistically; any hope of ultimate survival of our civilization depends on the social awareness and political participation of other segments of the public. Social awareness and political participation learning experiences <u>should</u> be the first priority on the agenda of life-long education.

2. Community institutions and organizations are the major loci of learning experiences with a social awareness and political participation focus, and should be treated as major partners in this activity.

3. Every adult learning experience has a political aspect, which should be made explicit.

4. Successful social awareness and political participation education requires an educational methodology of programming with, not programming for, adult learners.

5. Preretirement educational programming located in the work place, including sensitization to political participation, should become institutionalized.

6. The role of universities should be resource centres rather than merely providers of learning experience.

7. The role of government (other than with its own employees) should be to provide facilities, media vehicles, and funding of exploration of alternative

options in the face of our political choices.

8. Canadian television and radio should be liberated from the dominance of consumer propaganda.

9. Most organized life-long learning experiences which have social awareness and political participation goals are directed largely to the middle class, or to persons who are or have been in the economic mainstream of the country, while major groupings of people who are in an economically weak position (like most of the hundreds of thousands of women over age sixty-five) <u>do not</u> participate in such experiences. There is a dire need for pilot projects and resources to explore the feasibility of making the mainstream of life-long education genuinely accessible to such persons.

REFERENCES

Asimov, Isaac. *A Choice of Catastrophes* (New York: Fawcett Columbine, 1979).

Carroll, Eugene (Rear Admiral retired). Ottawa address, November 13, 1981 and subsequent interview by Gifford in Washington, D.C., December 7, 1981.

Carson, Rachel. *Silent Spring* (Houghton Mifflin, 1962).

Clark, Alan. *The Donkeys* (New York: Morrow, 1962).

DEA brochure. 121 Avenue Road, Toronto, Ontario.

Elderhostel Brochures, 1981, obtainable from regional (Atlantic) and provincial (Ontario and Quebec) coordinators.

Erdmann, Paul. *The Last Days of America* (New York: Simon and Schuster, 1981).

Fuller, R. Buckminster. *Utopia or Oblivion: The Prospects for Humanity* (Harmondsworth: Penguin Books, 1969).

Globe and Mail (Toronto, Nov. 28, 1981, p. 2).

Halberstam, David. *The Powers That Be* (New York: Dell, 1979).

Harriman, Averill. *The Manchester Guardian Weekly*, November 15, 1981;

Heilbroner, Robert L. *An Inquiry into the Human Prospect* (New York: W.W. Norton, 1974).

Lessing, Doris. *Children of Violence* (Bristol: MacGibbon and Kee, 1965).

Lessing, Doris. *The Four Gated City* (London: MacGibbon and Kee, 1969).

Lessing, Doris. *The Golden Notebook* (New York: Simon and Schuster, 1962).

MacLennan, Hugh. *Voices in Time* (Toronto: MacMillan, 1980).

Meadows, D. et al. *The Limits to Growth* (New York: New American Library, 1972).

Mesarovic, M.D. and Eduard Pestel. *Mankind at the Turning Point* (New York: Dutton, 1974).

Mishler, William. *Political Participation in Canada* (Toronto: Macmillan, 1979).

Murrow, Edward R. Quoted in David Halberstam, *The Powers That Be* (New York: Dell, 1979), pp. 214-215.

Oxfam-Canada pamphlet.

The Saskatchewan Senior, news report, 1980.

Senior Citizen: 1981 Fall Calendar. The University of Calgary, 1981.

Shute, Nevil. *On the Beach* (London: Heinemann, 1966).

TALA (Third Age Learning Associates). (Room 120, York Hall, 2275 Bayview Avenue, Toronto, Ontario, May 5, 1980).

TALNEWS. (Room 120, York Hall, 2275 Bayview Avenue, Toronto, Ontario, Fall, 1981).

Vacca, Roberto. *The Coming Dark Age* (St. Albans: Panther Books, 1974).

CHAPTER 9

PERSONAL FULFILLMENT PROGRAMS: A PRACTITIONER'S VIEW

Anne Ironside

Introduction

This chapter is about personal fulfillment programs, their movement over the past decade from a concern with self to a concern with relatedness, the values these programs have for participants, learners with learning resources, and their relevance to policy makers concerned with adult learning.

As systematic integrated data on personal fulfillment programs in Canada is almost totally lacking (with none at all kept on age, social class and ethnicity) this chapter is essentially the case study of planning non-credit, personal fulfillment programs at the University of British Columbia Continuing Education Department, augmented by experience from the Canadian Committee on Learning Opportunities for Women and the development of related educational policies in British Columbia.

Existing Canadian data is now obsolete and does not distinguish between programs of psycho-social development and programs of general interest. Both are called "personal fulfillment" but they have different social relevance in psycho-social development.

Although personal fulfillment programs are usually considered to be outside the interest of public policy makers, this chapter proposes (1) a new concept of personal fulfillment programs and (2) public funding of "life planning" learning centres.

Personal Fulfillment Programs: The Evolution of a Concept

Personal fulfillment programs are one outgrowth of North America's changing concept of self-fulfillment. In *The New Rules*, Daniel Yankelovich (1981) traces the change from a "self-denial" ethic, through a "duty-to-self" ethic to an ethic of "commitment" which emphasizes relatedness to the world. This latter shift has come about for two reasons: The "duty-to-self" ethic assumed that the problems of scarcity were solved (which was false) and "duty-to-self" was emotionally bankrupt. Yankelovich rejects the self as private, wholly encased in one's body because there is no "self" which can be separated from one's culture.

This shift from "duty-to-self" to "related to the world" is reflected by the evolution of personal fulfillment programs over the past decade.

A personal fulfillment program moves toward understanding one's self and one's relationship to society, and emphasizes the integration of factors that create life satisfaction: work that suits you, relationships that are satisfying, relatedness to the community, a sense of meaning and the energy to pursue one's activities with enthusiasm. These new personal fulfillment programs emphasize an _approach_ to life that includes all one does - including one's rights and duties as a citizen.

While these statements are true for men and women, they have special relevance for women's programs. From their origins in the late sixties, these women's programs have always aimed at establishing a new balance in the giving/getting contract, which underlies all life in any society.

Whether through nature or nurture, women see themselves primarily as givers in relationships. Because of these perceptions, self-fulfillment programs have always focussed on moving women toward establishing more equity in their relationships with others. Communication skills and assertiveness training have been important elements in these programs because they facilitate equity in relationships.

Besides the cultural shift in the giving/getting compact, three other important shifts have affected attitudes in personal fulfillment:

1. An awareness of the relationship between mind and body, of psyche and soma, which drew upon the exerience of centres like Esalen and Cold Mountain Institute. These approaches for mind/body integration are now part of adult education offerings, preventive medical practice, and are also having an impact on health promotion policy (Shifting Medical Paradigm, 1981).

2. Broadening "personal fulfillment" to include "work satisfaction." Recently there has been a growing awareness of the inter-relationship of work satisfaction, stress and longevity. Clients of personal fulfillment programs are looking for creative solutions to work satisfaction, either through job change, job enrichment or human relations skills which enable them to get on better with boss and co-workers.

3. An awareness of the need to change societal institutions to improve the _quality_ of relationships. Feminists have seen that personal fulfillment for women is impossible within the present social context. Women's personal fulfillment programs challenge the division between the domestic and the non-domestic sphere. Why? Well, to answer Freud's question of what do women want?, we want to love _and_ to work!

Program Participants

Participants in personal fulfillment programs tend to be middle class persons who are more aware of change and more willing to experiment. Without government support for such programs, poor families and individuals cannot afford experiments although they may be aware of the need for change.

Most of the clients have been touched by the "new consciousness" through contact with the women's movement, the environmental movement, the self-care health movement, or the human potential movement, all of which propose that although one's view of oneself and one's relation to the world has been conditioned, one can consciously choose a more appropriate view.

Judith Bardwick (1979) in researching middle class women in the U.S.A. says that women under 50 years of age are most likely to alter their lives in response to the ideas of these movements. Therefore, cohort theory may be more useful than developmental theory in predicting what will be happening to these 25-40 year olds in the future.

Although participants in the women's programs tend to be restricted to those who can afford their self-sustaining requirements, similar methods would be useful for low-income women if the course emphasis were shifted to practical solutions for pressing problems. Because some middle class women sense that they are only one man away from welfare, some of their interest in life/career planning may rest on their sense of insecurity.

Clients of the Women's Resources Centre life planning service provide a small sample of "hard data." There were 66 in the study, with ages ranging from 19 to 67 with a mean of 35.5. Seventy-two percent were between 19 and 40. Seventy percent were from Vancouver. Another recent program on personal transformation, open to men and women, had a median age of 43 years.

Program Values

Adult developmental theorists characterize adulthood as alternating between periods of stability and change. Life/career planning programs and services are particularly useful for people in transition. In the recent study of the University of British Columbia's Women's Resources Centre, 82% of women described themselves as being in transition. The people who reported receiving the most benefit were those who described themselves as being in a state of readiness for change (Fournier 1981).

Toombs has observed (1978) that "For adults it appears that education may have less intrinsic value but more instrumental importance." Fifty-five percent of our clients are most concerned about their immediate job situation and educational choices which relate to their job.

Participants in women's programs report an increase in self-confidence, receiving acceptance, encouragement of self-directedness, control of life direction, information about opportunities available to them and consciousness of women's issues and an understanding of how this affects their lives.

One of our most provocative findings is that 73% of our clients reported an improved ability to develop and utilize social networks. Is life satisfaction directly related to this ability to develop and utilize social networks?

Life Planning/Learning Centres as Educational Brokers

Program provision is not enough: learning centres are a desirable link between learners and learning resources (Cross 1978). Though widespread in the United States, there are few of these educational brokerages in Canada. In Vancouver, the Centre plays an essential role, with eleven thousand drop-in and phone-in contacts in 1980. This centre is the "listening ear" of programmers to the emerging needs of clients.

A number of social commentators have spoken of the need

for such centres. Toffler in _The Third Wave_ (1979) says that counsellors should stop rummaging around in peoples' _ids_ and _egos_ and develop life organizing centres. Elise Boulding (1981) speaks of the need for places where people can "craft a life path". Although many adults have negative attitudes to education, the informal atmosphere of the life planning centre is ideal in assisting women to reconsider the place of education in their lives.

A successful life planning learning centre has three important elements:

- educational information
- life/career planning peer counsellors
- informal classrooms

Our experience confirms Heffernan's (1980) research which shows that the most successful of the educational brokerage services operate with a comprehensive on-site counselling back-up.

Policy in Adult Education

What should governments do, given that adults can and need to learn? Should life-long learning be a privilege, a right or an obligation? I propose that:

1. Public funds should be allocated for those personal fulfillment programs and services that deal with life/career planning because of their socio-economic consequences.

2. Provincial and federal governments should develop policies that support but do not control adult learning.

3. In planning their priorities, all ministries should allocate an education budget for implementation of their policies.

In B.C., a policy was developed for Women's Access Centres based on our work in the UBC Women's Centre and the

Zimmerman/Trew report which examined women's patterns of participation in community colleges in that province. There are now seven access centres in post-secondary institutions and plans to fund 15 more.

Access centres which facilitate life/career planning for women are justified because women need to prepare themselves for labour market participation and a great deal of money is wasted when people drop out of training programs, either because of improper career choice or inadequate preparation for the multiple responsibilities of being student, worker and parent.

The Faris Commission in B.C. (1976) and the Jean Commission in Quebec (1980) have led the public discussion leading to the development of Canadian policy in adult education. Other provincial ministries of education have been uneven in their commitment to adult education or to the concept of public participation in its development. While it is important for governments to support adult education, consideration must be given to how the funding is done.

As any practitioner of adult education knows, the dynamism in the field is in the informal sector. Here programs succeed only when they are perceived to meet people's needs. Clients will only pay for programs when they feel the content will help them lead more satisfying lives. For many, institution based settings - unless they are informal - are not conducive to adult learning. Government funding must be allocated in such a way as to encourage the adult education which takes place in the informal sector.

Ministries should plan their activities with a systematic view of the inter-relationship of apparently separate activities. They need an educational allocation for the learning implications of their policies. The Self Care movement in health promotion provides a good example of this.

In 1974, Marc Lalonde issued a document called "A New Perspective on the Health of Canadians". It discussed health as the result of the interplay of four things: one's biology, the health care system, the physical environment, and lifestyle factors such as diet, exercise and ability to manage stress. Although the educational implications of this were obvious, there were not sufficient funds to re-educate the public. Integrated strategies should also have been worked out with Ministries of Labour and the Environment - or at least that health promotion departments should work closely with occupational health and safety departments. Instead, health promotion programs have tended to focus on factors such as diet, exercise and relaxation skills, over which an individual was assumed to have control. These programs promoted the idea that one could and should take responsibility for one's own health. Nevertheless, an individual has control over only about 25% of health risk factors and the major risks to health lie outside an individual's direct control (Labonte and Penfold 1981). This means that social responsibility and self-interest come together in the need for people to take responsibility for creating a healthy environment.

The combination of personal and social responsibility returns to the central theme of this chapter. Adults require learning experiences on the changing relationship of self to society. Personal fulfillment programs need to be seen primarily as programs in psycho-social development. It is in the public interest to fund these programs because of their socio-economic value to the development of Canadian society.

REFERENCES

Bardwick, J.M. *In Transition: How Feminism, Sexual Liberation, and the Search for Self-fulfillment Have Altered America* (New York: Holt, Rinehart and Winston, 1979).

Boulding, Elise. "The Place of the Family in Times of Transition: Imaging of Familial Future", Vancouver: Presentation of the Vanier Institute (1981).

Cross, P.A. *The Missing Link: Connecting Adult Learners to Learning Resources* (New York: College Entrance Examination Board, 1978).

Fournier, Rosemary. *Educational Brokering and the University of British Columbia Women's Resource Center: A Client Reaction Study* (Vancouver: Faculty of Education (unpublished M.A. thesis, 1981)).

Heffernan, J.M. *Educational and Career Services for Adults* (Lexington: D.C. Heath and Company, 1981).

Ironside, A. and Weinstein, M.S. (editors). *Shifting Medical Paradigm: From Disease Prevention to Health Promotion* (Conference Proceedings). (Vancouver: University of British Columbia, Adult and Continuing Education, 1981).

Ironside, A. "Women's Access Centres: A Proposal, Centre for Continuing Education," (Vancouver: The University of British Columbia, 1979).

Labonte, Ronald and Susan Penfold. "Canadian Perspectives in Health Promotion: A Critique," *Health Education Canada*, Vol. 19, Nos. 3,4, 1981, 4-9.

Lalonde, M. *A New Perspective on the Health of Canadians* (Ottawa: National Health and Welfare, April 1974).

Neidhardt, J.E., Weinstein, M.S., Conry, R.F. *Introduction to Stress and Stress Management*. Western Center for

Preventive and Behavioral Medicine, North Vancouver, B.C., 1980.

Toffler, A. *The Third Wave* (New York: William Morrow and Company, Inc., 1980).

Toombs, W. "A Study of Client Reactions: Lifelong Learning Center." Center for the Study of Higher Education, The Pennsylvania State University, May 1978.

U.S. Department of Health, Education and Welfare. *Work in America*, Report of a Special Task Force to the Secretary of Health, Education and Welfare (Cambridge, Mass.: M.I.T. Press, 1971).

Willis, J. "Learning Opportunities for Women - An Impressionistic Overview." Canadian Committee on Learning Opportunities for Women. (Available from the Canadian Association for Adult Education), Toronto, 1977.

Yankelovich, D. *New Rules: Searching for Self-fulfillment in a World Turned Upside Down* (New York: Random House, 1981).

Zimmerman, L. and Trew, M. "A Report on Non-Traditional Learning Programs for Women at B.C. Post-Secondary Institutions." Information Services, Province of B.C., Ministry of Education, Science and Technology, January 1979.

CHAPTER 10

VALUE ISSUES OF LIFELONG EDUCATION IN AN AGING SOCIETY

Michael D. Bayles

The educational characteristics of populations have long been reported by demographers. The emphasis is usually upon literacy and formal education -- what percentages have completed elementary, secondary, and post-secondary schooling. While these data are quite useful for some purposes, especially in less developed countries, they do not accurately picture the educational level of a population. The varied forms of education that most people receive during their lives -- from on-the-job training, agricultural extension programs, educational television, and other informal sources, for example -- are not tabulated, in part because it is virtually impossible to acquire the data in statistical form. Indeed, it is not even possible to collect complete data on continuing education courses offered by Canadian universities.

The aging of a society, such as Canada will continue to experience during the next half century, increases the importance of adult lifelong learning -- formal, non-formal and informal -- relative to that of the usual school-age population, 6-22 years old. As the usual school-age population declines or remains constant in size, pressure upon elementary, secondary, and post-secondary school facilities lessens. To a large extent, Canada has already experienced this change. While the decline or steady state of the usual formal schooling populations has been recognized and evaluated, little has been done to formulate policies with respect to lifelong education for mature adults.(1) Already in Canada, over 40% of the university enrolment consists of people over 25 years of age (Foot 1981, p. 45). As the population over 25 years of age increases in relative and absolute size, it will probably constitute a larger segment of university enrolment. It may have even greater significance for policy questions concerning lifelong education.

What implications does the aging of the Canadian population have for lifelong education policies? Answering this general question involves both fact and value. Among the factual considerations are projections of the sizes of various age groups, the current status of lifelong education, and the capacity of existing programs to expand to serve more people. But factual information does not settle policy. Value considerations are also involved. What is the value to the individual and society of various types of lifelong educaton? Is the provision of lifelong education a government responsibility, or should it be left to the private sector?

The primary function of this chapter is to identify some value-related policy questions which require further consideration. In doing so, a general framework is offered for addressing them. As a secondary aspect, some arguments are offered for government responsibility for lifelong education.

---

(1) 'Policies' is here not restricted to active funding or operating of programs by the government, but includes laissez-faire government policies (doing nothing) as well as various forms of indirect encouragement such as tax deductions for fees, etc. It also includes simply adopting a goal of making lifelong learning available to all.

Values

It is important to clarify the kinds of values being examined. The study of values can be descriptive or normative. A descriptive study analyzes the values held by people. Values in this sense are those things, conditions, or experiences which people desire. One cannot depend simply upon people's verbal reports of the values they hold. When questioned, especially in public, people may espouse values, such as racial equality, which they do not practically pursue. However, if one judges a person's values solely by his or her conduct, one might not obtain an accurate assessment of that person's values. Some conditions might be valued but not actually pursued simply because there is no opportunity to achieve them. For example, a person may want to become a physician but actually pursue a nursing career because sex or age discrimination or financial considerations prevent pursuit of a medical education. Thus, the priorities of values actually pursued are context dependent.

That the relative priority of values is context-dependent may be of special significance to lifelong education. The goals people have in education can differ with respect to their age, sex, marital, economic, and other statuses. The value of further vocational education is not the same for a newly trained 25-year-old male lawyer as for a recently divorced 42-year-old woman with a high school education and two teenage children. In general, insufficient information is available describing the values of various segments of the Canadian population with respect to lifelong education. First, there is inadequate information about the desires of people now in various age categories. Second, it cannot simply be assumed that the attitudes now held by persons over the age of 65 will be reflected in that age group two decades from now. Indeed, since those persons over 65 years of age in 2001 will be better educated than at present, they are apt to want proportionately more educational opportunities. Third, the life experiences of various cohorts can significantly affect their attitudes towards, and desires for, lifelong education.

The normative study of values does not describe the

values people hold, but rationally examines them. It
analyzes what will indeed be beneficial to persons or
society. Although considerable philosophical dispute exists
as to whether such analysis can be performed, let alone how
it should be done, some possibilities for such analysis are
generally recognized. If certain general values are accepted
or given, one can analyze subordinate ones. Thus, if life
and health are accepted as valuable, health care can be shown
to be a reasonable subordinate value. Similarly, if an
informed electorate is valuable, then literacy is also
valuable.

In formulating social policies, normative value
assessment is often involved. For example, in setting
television and radio broadcast policy, the government does
not decide simply on the basis of the values held by a
majority of the population. Certain content requirements of
Canadian and public affairs are set on the grounds that they
are beneficial even if people do not fully realize it. In
education, such judgments are common. Elementary school
curricula are not determined on the basis of the values
expressed or held by the students, but from normative
judgments as to what is most beneficial for students and
society. As students advance through school, they are
allowed more freedom to choose their curriculum.
Nevertheless, even in graduate school, certain requirements
are set on the basis of normatively justified values.

However, it is an open question whether lifelong
education curricula should be determined by students or
should be guided by rational assessments of what would be
most valuable for people. Of course, the choice is not an
either/or one; various mixes are possible. For example,
student demand could determine the courses or programs to be
offered, and rational assessments could determine the more
detailed aspects of curriculum. Moreover, this might vary
for different types of education. Thus, it may be more
reasonable to set basic curricula for vocational and
technical training by rational assessment, but allow general
interest and leisure curricula to respond to public demand.
It might also make sense for the government to support only
those forms of lifelong education which are normatively

beneficial to society. Thus, normative assessment of the values of lifelong education is essential to the formulation of social policy concerning it.

In both the descriptive and normative study of values, two distinctions are quite important. The first distinction is between intrinsic and instrumental values. Intrinsic values are those which are desirable for their own sake, not for the sake of things to which they might lead. Instrumental values are those which are valuable for the sake of that to which they lead. Happiness, for example, is usually thought to be intrinsically valuable; it does not make much sense to seek happiness for the sake of something else, for to what could it lead that would be more worth having. Money is usually of only instrumental value; it is not valuable in itself but for the things one can purchase with it. Of course, many things have both types of value; they are worth having for their own sake as well as for their outcomes. Knowledge is often thought to have both types of value. In analyzing the values of lifelong learning, it is important to consider whether they are primarily intrinsic or instrumental.

The second distinction is between individual and social values. Individual values are those which benefit an individual; social values are those which benefit society. Although there is much philosophical debate as to whether social values can be defined in terms of individual values, for purposes of this discussion they are assumed to be distinct. The primary justification for this assumption is that no close connection exists between benefit to society and to all individuals in it. An increase in the real national product may benefit society, although certain individuals lose rather than gain, for example, people displaced by new technologies.

Values in Lifelong Education

Values and issues underlying lifelong education vary depending upon the type of education. Each of the four types in the overall study -- for literacy, for vocational and technical skills, for social and political awareness, and for personal fulfillment -- is examined separately. In the concluding section, some more general and comparative issues are raised.

Literacy. The instrumental value of literacy for individuals is rarely denied. Numerical and reading skills are essential for independent functioning in modern industrial societies. Without these abilities, persons cannot conduct banking, read job want ads, know whether they receive correct change, or understand various regulations. Moreover, literacy is necessary for most but not all other forms of education; people unable to read and write can develop a deep understanding of other people and society.

The intrinsic value of literacy to individuals is somewhat less clear. Is it valuable in itself to be able to read and write? Here one must be clear what education involves. Essentially, it develops a person's capacities into trained abilities. For example, a person has the capacity to learn French, and after instruction has the ability to speak and read it. One can also distinguish between having an ability and exercising it. In considering the intrinsic value of education, one considers the value inherent in the exercise of learned abilities and ignores the value of the consequences of using those abilities. Thus, for literacy one considers the value in reading or numerical calculation, not the value of consequences such as being able to obtain jobs. Reading and writing are often intrinsically valuable activities. Perhaps few people write merely because they enjoy doing so, but reading for pleasure is a common activity. One can see recognition of the intrinsic value of reading as children become able to read on their own. There is the happy look when they first master what previously were difficult sentences or sound out polysyllabic words. Some of this joy stems from accomplishment of a difficult task, but that is not always the sole satisfaction.

The instrumental value of a literate population for society is also undeniable. A literate population constitutes a more skilled labour force capable of producing more goods and services, often at less cost. One should not confuse a literate labour force with a capital-intensive rather than labour-intensive economy. In Canada, a literate labour force working in capital-intensive conditions is well established. Capital-intensive developments like robots and microcomputers are now eliminating many of the jobs which have not required literacy. Another and distinct consequence of a literate population is its ability to respond to government requests. Although modern Canadian government would be inconvenienced if most of the population were incapable of reading various materials such as income tax and census forms, the development of radio and television has perhaps decreased the importance of this aspect, since much communication can now be verbal.

A more difficult question is whether a literate population has intrinsic social value. If society is better simply because it has a certain characteristic, then that characteristic has intrinsic social value. Because of the freedoms people have, Canada is a better society than it would be if there were fewer freedoms. That is, a free society is intrinsically better than an unfree one. The question is whether a literate society is for that reason alone better or more valuable than an illiterate one. Here it is difficult to distinguish whether literacy is intrinsically valuable or only instrumentally valuable. For example, is a literature included in the very notion of, or is it a consequence of, a literate society? If one does not assume the literature is very good and recognizes that preliterate societies were populated by storytellers and others who preserved culture, then it may be difficult to argue that literacy is an intrinsic social value. The conceptual framework of a literate society probably differs significantly from a nonliterate one, but that need not make it better.

If the social value of literacy is instrumental, then there are some implications for lifelong education. Functional illiteracy correlates with length of time since formal schooling (as well as amount of formal schooling). This suggests that in an aging population there may be more illiterate older people, a trend that may be counteracted by the increasingly high levels of formal education of Canada's elderly. But if the social value of literacy is instrumental in training a work force and other such aspects, then there is little social value in providing literacy education for people over age 55. As the remaining period in which they are employed (one measure of contributing to society) decreases, the social benefit which would be derived from their becoming literate also decreases.

This same issue of declining value also pertains to the value of literacy to individuals. Insofar as one focuses on the instrumental value of literacy for independent living in society, then it too might decrease with age. However, there is at least one serious reservation on this point. Many illiterate people manage in society because they have literate spouses who handle their affairs. If a literate spouse dies when both are, say, 63 years old, then considerable instrumental value stems from the surviving illiterate spouse learning to read and write.

None of these considerations about the instrumental value of literacy affects its intrinsic individual value. Many retired persons learn to read and write simply because they want to be able to do so. The value contained in reading for pleasure is not age restricted; elderly and retired persons, who are often limited with respect to physical recreation, can find much enjoyment and value in reading. However, one must consider the extent to which it is a government responsibility to provide people with opportunities to engage in such intrinsically valuable activities. This issue will be discussed more fully in considering education for personal fulfillment.

Vocational and Technical. The instrumental value of vocational and technical education for individuals is obvious. By definition, such education is oriented to developing job skills and enabling people to obtain employment or advancement. Employment is not only a source of income but a source of personal identity. Most people partially define themselves by their employment -- as secretaries, engineers, lawyers, nurses, teachers, plumbers, and so on. The importance of employment for personal identity seems weaker for women than men, in part because many women relate strongly to their family role. It is not clear whether this difference will continue if women spend proportionately more of their lives in the work force. However, there is also intrinsic value in such education, or at least in the exercise of skills and abilities gained through it. Most people find enjoyment in activities which they do well and which involve more complex abilities and skills (Rawls 1971, p. 426). Thus, people are apt to find work which involves such activities intrinsically valuable and part of what makes their lives meaningful and worth living.

The instrumental social value of vocational and technical education is much the same as that of literacy, but it is even more directly related to a skilled labour force. Vocational and technical education has little instrumental social value if it is directed at jobs for which there already exists a surplus of trained workers. Whether such education has any intrinsic social value is much the same question as whether there is intrinsic social value in a literate population. Insofar as vocational and technical education is by definition job-related, it is even less plausible that it has intrinsic social value. The great instrumental social value usually makes the question of intrinsic social value otiose.

Two rather obvious implications of an aging society relate to vocational and technical education. First, as women have fewer children and their labour force participation increases, their demand for lifelong vocational and technical training increases. Many women in their thirties and early forties who withdrew from the labour force to raise (or at least start) families are seeking vocational and technical training to renew old skills or obtain new ones. They are also completing formal schooling interrupted for the same reason. As this segment of the population becomes proportionately larger, demand for such education will increase.

A second aspect of an aging population is connected with rapid technological development. With rapid technological change, job skills learned in the late teens and early twenties can become obsolete by middle age. In the past, Canada and other countries have implicitly relied upon new labour force entrants to be trained in the new skills needed, such as computer programming. In part, the large number of new entrants needed jobs, and they had to be given some form of training anyway. However, as a population ages, proportionately fewer persons will be entering the labour force and perhaps proportionately more will find their skills unneeded due to technological change. In this context, supplying workers with the new skills must increasingly depend upon immigration of trained workers and re-education of those who have been displaced. Thus, lifelong vocational and technical education will become more important in supplying needed skills in the labour force. Also, with rapid technological change and the obsolescence of skills, training older workers will have almost as much economic value as training new entrants. There are also questions of fairness in allowing displaced workers to flounder in society when they could be retrained.

Social and Political. The instrumental value to individuals of social and political education is more diffuse than that of literacy and vocational and technical education, but nonetheless important. Only if people understand their political system and social environment can they effectively pursue their interests. Citizens need to understand their rights if they are to protect and exercise them. Much that affects people results from political decisions and social changes. One need only consider a few of the many factors that can significantly affect people to realize the value of such education -- human rights commissions; tax, property, estate, contract, and family law; social welfare agencies; the educational system; and energy policy.

Social and political awareness can also be of considerable intrinsic value to individuals. By increasing their awareness and understanding of political institutions and society, it can make their lives more meaningful by placing them in the social context. A common feature of older generations is a feeling of being lost in society. Life is no longer as it was when they grew up; society is strange and bewildering. Lifelong education can provide an understanding of contemporary society and help people feel more at home in it as they age.

Insofar as Canada relies upon an informed and active electorate for adequate functioning, social and political education has significant instrumental social value. Politically and socially aware citizens can take a more enlightened and active role in society. Moreover, social and political education appears to have intrinsic social value. If government by the people rather than by bureaucracy is an intrinsically desirable form of government, then a more politically aware citizenry has more intrinsic value. Some people also consider participatory democracy to be intrinsically desirable, although that assumption can be seriously challenged (Bayles 1977). To the extent that participation is intrinsically valuable, the use of political and social knowledge in participation is intrinsically of social value.

The aging of Canadian society raises several issues for lifelong political and social education. First, if immigration is increased to supplement the work force, then appropriate education would be beneficial in integrating immigrants into Canadian life. Currently, no formal system exists to provide such education to immigrants. Some communities help. Highly educated immigrants can perhaps attain it by reading on their own, but others are less apt to do so.

Second, in general, older citizens are more active politically. That is, they have higher rates of participation in elections and take a more active role in political parties. As the Canadian society ages, one might expect a more politically and socially active population. If people are to be active, then they need to understand and be aware of social and political matters. Increased participation by unenlightened persons could be detrimental rather than beneficial to society.

Third, migration as well as immigration creates a need for social and political education. For example, schools teach the social history and operation of the governments of that province, but very little about other provinces. As people move for employment or other reasons, they could benefit from social and political education pertaining to provincial and local government and society. In this context, one should not ignore the movement of persons when they retire. Although most persons do not move then, a significant number do seek a more desirable climate or other features. Given the political activity of elderly persons and their time available for educational activities, regions which attract many retired persons, e.g., Victoria, may find a high demand and need for political and social education.

Fourth, social awareness might become especially important for particular segments of the population. In recent years, women's rights and feminism have been topics of particular concern. However, as the percentage of the population over 55 years of age increases, one might expect a significant increase in the demand for (and the value of) education for social awareness of the aged and their problems. Immigrant groups and structurally unemployed persons in their late thirties and early forties may also be targets for specialized programs.

Finally, education for social and political awareness can take many forms. During the early 1970s, East Germany adopted a new criminal code. As part of the process of adopting it, the proposed code was discussed at factories and other places of employment throughout the country. Whether or not the people had an effective role in shaping the proposed legislation, these widespread discussions significantly educated the population about the criminal law. The public discussion concerning patriation of the constitution may have served a similar function in Canada.

Personal Fulfillment. Just as the concept of vocational and technical education makes its instrumental value dominant, so the concept of education for personal fulfillment renders its intrinsic value dominant. The idea is to provide people with opportunities to develop skills and to engage in activities which they find rewarding. As with vocational and technical education, most people enjoy engaging in activities that they can perform reasonably well and that require the use of more, rather than less, complex abilities and skills. Many forms of personal fulfillment education also have instrumental value for individuals. Dancing is not only enjoyable in itself but beneficial to one's health. Some personal fulfillment education may be almost completely oriented to instrumental values, such as learning about automobile mechanics and personal health. However, many people who take a noncredit course in automobile mechanics and learn to change the oil in their cars find the minor tinkering with their automobiles a pleasant pastime, as well as a way of saving money.

The social value of education for personal fulfillment is less clear. It has some instrumental social value. If most people find their lives personally fulfilling, then there will be less social tension and disharmony. Physical recreation and personal health can also be significant factors in keeping the population healthy, thereby decreasing health care costs and days lost from work. It is difficult to distinguish the intrinsic social value of personal fulfillment education from its individual intrinsic value. Personal fulfillment at the social level simply consists in the fulfillment of the individuals in that society. So interpreted, however, personal fulfillment education has considerable intrinsic social value. Surely a society in which many of the people find their lives personally meaningful and fulfilling is better than one in which few or none do.

A question which needs to be examined in more detail is whether the aging of the Canadian society will make education for personal fulfillment more important. It is plausible to argue that personal fulfillment education is better the younger one is, because then one has more of life to engage in activities learned. However, as the importance of values is context-dependent, personally fulfilling activities might have less relative importance for younger adults than older ones. From the ages of 25 to 45, many people are establishing their careers and founding families. These activities might take priority over others that would be seen as personally fulfilling leisure activities. By the time people are 55 years old, their careers have usually peaked and their children grown up, or at least no longer require as much parental time. Moreover, as people retire they have more time to engage in personally fulfilling leisure activities, making a plausible argument for the increased importance of education for personal fulfillment as people age. As the segment of the population aged 55 years and over becomes larger, personal fulfillment education should become more important in society. However, one also needs a descriptive study of people's values as they mature, to see whether they do shift toward a greater importance of personally fulfilling activities.

Perhaps the central concern with education for personal fulfillment is whether it is an appropriate concern for government. One can argue that if people find the education fulfilling, they will be willing to pay for it. Thus, it can be provided through the private sector. Many dance studios exist, and one can easily envision privately run education centres for a variety of other activities. Moreover, government cannot do everything. It simply cannot provide satisfactory and fulfilling lives for people. Personal fulfillment education has little instrumental social value, so there is less social benefit from it than from education for literacy and vocational skills.

Four contrary considerations can be given in favour of government support for, and provision of, personal fulfillment education. First, to focus upon the instrumental benefit of programs is a mistake. Instrumental value is not in itself more of a governmental responsibility than intrinsic value. One does not claim that government should ignore programs fostering justice because justice is not instrumentally valuable. The mistaken emphasis upon instrumental value probably comes from overemphasis of economic benefit, to the neglect of other benefits. Although economic benefit is more easily quantifiable than the social benefit of people who lead personally fulfilling lives, it is not for that reason more important. Indeed, economic benefit is of value only if it promotes intrinsic values, such as personal fulfillment. At present, the policies of government and educational institutions appear to be on divergent paths. Governments are increasingly emphasizing education for instrumental purposes, while educational institutions appear to be returning to their traditional emphasis upon education for its own sake (intrinsic value). This divergence could well become central to policy decisions concerning lifelong education. Second, the government does undertake support of many programs chiefly concerned with personal fulfillment. Support of the arts primarily has that benefit, as does much liberal arts education in colleges and universities. Third, even if much personal fulfillment education can be provided through the private sector, a question of equality of opportunity arises. Not all Canadians can afford private sector programs. Of course, this concern could be addressed by government programs to improve the financial position of poorer Canadians. Finally, much of the talent for personal fulfillment education is located in government-funded educational institutions. Many of the persons most capable of teaching music, art, and literature appreciation are in the educational institutions. Thus, any large-scale offering of personal fulfillment education will have to draw upon this talent pool. In sum, government does support some personal fulfillment education; its intrinsic value can be as great as the instrumental value of other forms of education; government support is probably necessary to make it equally available; and government-funded institutions contain much of the talent needed for providing it.

General Value Issues

In conclusion, a few general value issues that require further investigation will be raised.

(1) What should be the relative priority of lifelong education versus early formal education and other programs? Perhaps the aging of the Canadian population will imply a shift of resources from early formal schooling to adult education. However, the aging of the population will also affect other sectors, such as health care and pensions. Some people have suggested that funds and resources can be shifted from education to health care and pensions as the demand and need for the latter increase. However, if the demand and need for lifelong education increase, perhaps there will be

labour force growth towards the end of the period. Little improvement is expected for unemployment which may average about 10% for the projection period, underlying the allocation of limited resources.

-- **Labour Productivity:** will increase at a rate just below 1½% per annum for the early years with possibly some improvement from 1985 and levels will remain below past and the potential performance. This requires a more detailed consideration of the descriptive and normative values of each type of population segment, both in combined, Moreover, it requires identifying the concerned by the federal government's 6 and 5% ruling. Even if the program extends to other sectors of the economy, the real wage will fall the projected 1985 and 1984, with some improvement in succeeding years of different cohorts.

-- **Personal Savings:** changes in personal savings have been a major factor in both containing inflation and various retarding business profits and employment levels. In 1982 personal savings were about 13.1%, compared to 10% over 1976-80. The rate of savings appeared to have risen both as a buffer against inflation and as a consequence of higher levels of assessment of the value of the difference between the nominal rate of interest and the rate of inflation. For example, the Canadian population changes.

-- **Government Receipts and Expenditures:** needs have been contained by a lower level of GNP and certainties participated then and the underpinning of the income structure by the "baby-boom" generation. Both had the effect of reducing government receipts, while unemployment also increased government expenditures through unemployment insurance and welfare programs. Debt servicing charges, associated with the high federal deficits will continue to exert upward pressure on government debt.

-- **Current Account Balance of International Payments:** allowed may improve slightly due to Canada's energy resources and the contraction of Canadian in relation to demands on the population. However, much will depend upon US rates of growth over future years since Canada's economy has become increasingly dependent upon the US. The expected US rate of growth from 1983 to 1987 is about 3%. The policies for

(6) To what extent should efforts be made to make lifelong learning opportunities equally available to all Canadians? Programs for people in rural and isolated places are less cost effective than those in large metropolitan areas. However, simply providing programs on the most cost effective basis will deny some Canadians opportunities enjoyed by others. Is it justifiable to deny some people opportunities for pesonal fulfillment or literacy simply because they reside in geographically isolated areas? Perhaps some of these concerns can be met by innovative and imaginative methods of lifelong education.

More thought should be given to various strategies for implementing lifelong education beyond those currently used or envisioned. For example, as the number of retired persons increases, perhaps some of them could be involved in teaching. Many people over 65 years are still quite active and have many talents and abilities which they can communicate to others. One can envision a future in which a much larger population of people over 55 years becomes a new learning community, not being taught by other persons, but sharing with each other what they have learned through their lives and experiences. Such a development might give meaning and fulfillment to many elderly people and help overcome the isolation and loneliness currently experienced by far too many of Canada's elderly. The potential exists for a significant blossoming of learning and life for an aging population. However, it will only be realized if imaginative and well-founded social policies are adopted. Before such policies are adopted, a more detailed consideration of the values of lifelong learning and their policy implications should be undertaken.

REFERENCES

Bayles, Michael D. "Participation: An Overvalued, Impractical Ideal," in *Equality and Freedom*, ed. Gray Dorsey, vol. 1 (Dobbs Ferry, N.Y.: Oceana Publications, 1977), pp. 351-57.

Foot, David K. "A Troubled Future? University Enrolments in Canada and the Province," in *Financing Canadian Universities: For Whom and By Whom?*, ed. David M. Nowlan and Richard Bellaire (Toronto: OISE Press, 1981), Table 5, pp. 45.

Rawls, John. *A Theory of Justice* (Cambridge: Harvard University Press, 1971), pp. 426-33.

CHAPTER 11

CONCLUSIONS AND RECOMMENDATIONS

Douglas Ray and Janet Collins

Towards a Better Understanding of Life-Long Education

Earlier chapters have discussed particular aspects of the study of life-long education but several conclusions address the project as a whole. They include difficulties to be faced, problems of definition and terminology, paradigm inadequacies and constraints of time and resources.

The Problem of Definition

Although the concept of life-long education is officially approved by Canadian educators and policy makers, it is variously and often vaguely defined, with no consistent distinction between life-long education and adult education or continuing education. For some, adult education is considered to be either recreational or a means of compensating for previous shortcomings. Others see it as vocationally oriented, especially at the technical or professional levels. However the basic philosophy of life-long education is that learning occurs throughout life, in different ways and through different processes (Bruner and

Olson 1973), so all individuals ought to have opportunities
for instruction, study and learning throughout life. Some
examples of individual goals may be to remedy earlier
education defects, to acquire new skills, to achieve
vocational upgrading, to develop their own personalities or
to increase their understanding of the world in which they
live. The excellent definitions and discussion of
authorities like Skager (1978) are not well known or
reflected in all policies.

Learning and Aging - a Psychological Viewpoint

Intellectual functioning has been assumed to vary with
age: for example, intellectual growth occurs in the young,
it peaks relatively early and is followed by a plateau and a
decline in later years. Although there is no agreement on
the precise ages at which these changes occur; on the shape
of the learning curve, there is general agreement. Recent
reviews of the literature have led to a more cautious
interpretation of the results of tests of intellectual
ability, and some authors have cautioned that not all
intellectual abilities decline with age. Some abilities may
not decline at all, while others may begin to decline much
later than previously thought. There is also the problem of
individual variation (Horn and Donaldson 1976).

These studies explain why performance of the elderly in
specific tasks varies with the circumstances of the test
(Welford 1969). They raise the possibility that learning in
adults is influenced by the appropriateness of instruction
and performance conditions. Thus the techniques of youth
instruction are not appropriate for those of advancing years
and new ways must be utilized to mobilize and organize
abilities. This argument strongly supports the view that
education should be life-long, since with advancing age new
approaches to problems become necessary, such as structuring
learning opportunities according to the changing nature of
intellectual abilities.

Cohort studies have become important. Although a static
paradigm might suggest that analysis of sixty year olds today

could predict the intellectual performance of today's youth when they reach sixty, cohort theory would emphasize the important differences that separate these two generations, including the difference in opportunities to learn. In fact, longitudinal studies in which the same group of individuals was tested 25 years apart showed no decline in ability (Campbell 1965), although the changing skills, abilities and needs of the aging merit continual up-dating and re-educating or life-long education.

Life-Long Education in Canada: Educational and Social Policies

Many groups have advocated, planned, or delivered educational services that contribute to the goal of life-long education. These groups represent a cross section of the education community: professional and volunteer, formal and non-formal, government and private sector agencies. A preliminary survey of six provinces assessed the services available to potential life-long students. The provincial Departments of Education were asked to provide any existing policy statements on life-long education, and any data which would indicate current progress toward this goal. Although the responses of these governments and data obtained from Statistics Canada give some indication of the present situation, the picture remains incomplete even for the provinces surveyed.

Present practice usually requires that adult students should pay for their own education, probably through fees reflecting the actual cost of the course. Although financial straits of students are rarely the basis for waiving the fees, there are some reorientation grants: i.e., assistance is more or less limited to vocational fields. It is probable that some poor families are unable or unwilling to make the required financial sacrifice, however much they might need or want the education. Private and public courses face similar financial obstacles so their services are not fully available to those with greatest need.

The large public expenditures for schooling, colleges,

universities and initial vocational training leaves little for life-long education. In effect the policy makers at both the provincial and local level deny the principle of life-long education. Similarly, the preoccupation of teachers with initial education makes them competitors for funding of life-long education.

Although the conventional wisdom holds that additional funding for schooling would be unpopular, it may be the most desirable of several choices. For example, funding of well run and effective life-long programs might well prove economic and popular. Voluntary contributions and exchange economy support for certain kinds of life-long educaton have not been properly evaluated, but recognizing appropriate instruction and/or credentials might bring many underground economic activities into the market place, with attendant benefits to taxation and opportunities to protect against unscrupulous practices (Livingstone and Hart 1981).

None of the provincial departments contacted in this study has clearly endorsed the principle of life-long education. Instead, there is no consensus on the nature and desirability of life-long education as a general goal. Notwithstanding major recommendations which have received widespread consideration and endorsement by provincially appointed commissions, in B.C., Alberta, Manitoba, Ontario, and Quebec, provincial departments of education have been slow to implement these recommendations. For example, although the British Columbia committee in 1976 recommended life-long learning as being basic to the planning of the public educational system, the 1980 educational policy statement reflects no radical shift (Province of British Columbia 1981).

In Ontario, the provincial department of education has published an interim report on continuing education (Province of Ontario 1981). One proposed goal is to clarify and to choose from different significant approaches to life-long education advocated by international bodies, e.g., recurrent education, permanent education and life-long education as defined in the 1972 UNESCO report, *Learning to Be* (Faure 1972).

Quebec at present has no formal system of continuing education accessible to everyone. The interim report of the commission studying adult education in Quebec recommended that legislation be enacted to give adults the right to education and other recommendations of the commission indicate a preference for life-long education (Commission d'étude 1981).

If provinces do not clearly endorse the principle of life-long education and back their endorsements with programs, they will and should vacate the field for federal training and citizenship activities.

Access to Data

Several problems in obtaining sufficiently detailed data for this study emerged. The federal publications of educational statistics, once reputed to be among the best in the world, have now discontinued many series of data and rising prices have made them less accessible as libraries cut back. Certain trends can no longer be followed and recent changes may go undetected. Provincial governments do not assume this educational responsibility; many of them have not gathered the necessary data and made it readily accessible. The best available data, although somewhat impressionistic and not consistent in certain categories, is gathered from individual centers (it is their in-house data) or from studies that reflect concerns similar to ours. Finally, there are the gut reactions of those in the field.

This study established that certain kinds of data are inaccessible, missing or incomplete - for example, several kinds of statistics are available from only certain provinces or institutions. This seems a remarkable oversight in a society where six million persons are full time students in schools and higher education. Moreover, there are several million more with important educational needs, many of these being taught with success in private sector programs or by informal means. The size and success of this formal/non formal/informal education remains incompletely charted. It is noted that life-long educaton is now provided by governments (federal, provincial and municipal), by non government voluntary agencies (YMCA, etc.), by private corporations or in the burgeoning economic exchange market. The inadequacies of this system are reflected in various statistics (e.g., illiteracy, structural unemployment), but the solutions proposed from time to time appear to be band-aids (Organization for Cooperation and Development 1976, pp. 89-103).

Examples of data sought for this study but secured only partially and with difficulty reflect the problem which would inhibit either researchers or policy makers.

1. Enrolments by type of course (literacy, technical, political and social, personal fulfillment).

2. The age and sex of students.

3. Policies concerning divisions of responsibility between public and non-governmental organizations. In some cases we were advised there was no policy. In others the policy was clear but not yet effective.

4. Trends in funding of various types of programs. The best series of data appear to be from Employment and Immigration Canada.

5. Titles or examples of in-house studies likely to impinge on this work.

6. Names of those persons likely to be able to provide any of this data.

The best data was often obtained from individual program directors and their personal networks, not from the departments nominally responsible. Apparently life-long education is a shoe string operation in most cases, with the personal determination of organizers and manipulation of opportunities more significant to success than clear policy and adequate systems to accomplish it.

There is a need for systematic organization of information as a prelude to decisions concerning programs.

LIFE-LONG EDUCATION - MEETING FUTURE NEEDS

Three broad changes are necessary in educational institutions if the needs of an aging population are to be met: (1) Attitudes to learning, (2) meeting the need where it is greatest and (3) defining the roles of various formal, informal and non-formal agencies of education. These discussions are summarized below.

1. Attitudes to Learning - Values

Legislators, educators and the general public must decide if a particular form of education is a right or a privilege. At present it is universally agreed that children have a right to education. For adults there is no agreement. Although a few jurisdictions lean toward universal rights for old and young, even in those provinces where legislation exists, equal access may be denied by other restrictions, like poverty or remoteness.

Attitudes to learning are influenced by other factors besides perceived rights. The prevalent notion that intellectual ability declines with age has deterred many who might desire and profit from life-long education. It is essential that, beginning with school-age population and throughout life, educators instill and reinforce the possibility of learning throughout life. Moreover, it is imperative that educators recognize the importance for them to acquire competence in teaching methods appropriate for the practice of life-long education.

2. Meeting the Need Where it is Greatest - Access

Who gets education? A recurrent theme in discussions of life-long education, however defined, is that those with the highest level of education are apt to take advantage of opportunities for further learning. Considerations of equity suggest that help should be given to those who need most to upgrade their education. Some factors affecting variation in need are: low educational attainment (e.g., early school leaving), age, ethnicity, sex, attitudes to learning. The problem is not only to increase the motivation of such individuals to seek life-long education, but to ensure that their needs are appropriately met.

Age. Equity also requires access to retraining for older workers (for example, those over 45) and for those already employed (there are already well-established albeit imperfect schemes for the unemployed). As the population ages, the proportion of older workers needing retraining will obviously increase, and as already recognized by such studies as Adams' (1979), adults should have reasonable opportunities throughout life to improve their qualifications and prepare for alternative occupations.

Sex. The analysis of economic outlook shows sex to be a highly significant factor in determining need as older women are likely to be differently affected by changes in the age profile of the working population. It is projected that demand for older women workers will increase after 2001, because younger workers, both male and female, will be in short supply. It will consequently be essential that appropriate life-long educational opportunities exist to maintain the required level of skills in a rapidly changing technological environment.

Ethnicity. The Council of Ministers of Education in Canada's report to an OECD conference on "Policies for Higher Education in the 1980's" listed ethnicity as a disadvantage affecting individual access to higher education. Racism would be more so. Within an aging Canadian population there will be a significant ethnic, non-white segment for whom special effort must be made if their original educational deficits are to be overcome. This is most serious for the Native population which is projected to increase its proportion in the aging population (see p. 36).

3. The Role of the Formal and Informal Systems of Education

Who provides? Strategies for organizing a life-long educational system should be like those advocated by UNESCO in the Faure report (1972). These views emerged in relation to two primary questions:

1. What should be the roles of the formal and informal systems of education in providing life-long

education?

2. What should be the sources of funding and in what proportion?

Although there is no centralized store of data on the identity of private and public voluntary organizations that provide opportunities for adult learning and the types of courses of study offered, these quite obviously make a significant contribution that will continue in some form. This choice or competition of public and private sources facilitates the flexibility considered desirable for learners to choose what they will learn, as well as when and in what setting.

The reluctance of local and provincial governments and of private business to support the financial costs of life-long education programs probably stems from their realization that many benefits of such education may accrue to another region or another firm. Mobility is high for those with skills and self-assurance. The solution may be for senior government to increase its role either by payments (educational vouchers perhaps) directly to the student, or by tax concessions to corporations, both public and private, that offer approved educational services.

RECOMMENDATIONS

1. An effective means of gathering, recording and reporting data on all kinds of education should be developed. At present the system emphasizes school, college and university full-time programs. Private education by NGO, individuals and other enterprises is barely recorded and often unacknowledged.

2. Better coordination among various authorities (e.g., public/private, various levels of government, parallel agencies at the same level) should be given priority.

3. Policy decisions affecting life-long education like access despite poverty or isolation need to be set, with progressive implementation then possible.

4. Migration of populations must be anticipated in determining funding responsibilities.

REFERENCES

Adams, R.J. et al. *Education and Working Canadians*. Report of the Commission of Inquiry on Educational Leave and Productivity, 1979.

Advance Statistics of Education 1981-82 (Ottawa: Statistics Canada, 1981).

Bruner, J.S. and Olson, D.R. "Learning through experience and learning through media", *Prospects: Quarterly Review of Education*, 1973, 3:20-38.

Campbell, D.P. "A cross-sectional and longitudinal study of scholastic abilities over twenty-five years", *Journal of Counselling Psychology*, 1965, 12:55-61.

Commission d'étude sur la formation professionelle et socio-culturelle des adultes. Adult Education in Quebec: Possible Solutions. A work document, 1981.

Council of Ministers of Education, Canada. *Aspects of Post-Secondary Education in Canada*, 1981.

Faure, E. et al. *Learning to be. The world of education today and tomorrow*. UNESCO, Paris, 1972.

Horn, J.L. and Donaldson, G. "On the myth of intellectual decline in adulthood", *American Psychologist*, 1976, 31:701:719.

Livingstone, D.W. and Hart, D.J. *Public Attitudes Toward Education in Ontario, 1980* (Toronto: Ontario Institute for Studies in Education, 1981).

Organization for Economic Co-operation and Development, *Reviews of National Policies for Education*, (Paris: OECD, 1976).

Province of British Columbia, Ministry of Education. A Ministerial Policy on the Provision of Community Education and General Interest Education Programs in the Public Educational System of British Columbia, 1981.

Province of British Columbia. "Report of the Committee on Continuing and Community Education in British Columbia", 1976.

Province of Manitoba. *Post-Secondary Education in Manitoba*. Report of the Task Force on Post-Secondary Education in Manitoba, 1973.

Province of Ontario, Ministry of Education. Ministry of Colleges and Universities, "Continuing Education: The Third System". A discussion paper, 1981.

Skager, R. *Lifelong Education and Evaluation Practice* (Toronto: Pergamon, 1978), pp. 5-7.

Welford, A.T. "Age and Skill: Motor, intellectual and social", *Interdisciplinary Topics in Gerontology*, 1969, 4:1-22.

Worth, W.H. et al. *A Choice of Futures*. Report of the Commission on Educational Planning (Edmonton: Queen's Printer, Alberta, 1972).

BIBLIOGRAPHY

Compiled by Janet Collins, Jeanette Tran and Douglas Ray

Aids to Researchers

Anderson, Etel E.; Thomas, Audrey M. and Youssef, C. *Directory of Adult Basic Education Programs in Canada* (Toronto: The Movement for Canadian Literacy, 1978).

Rancier, Gordon and Brooke, M.W. *An Annotated Bibliography of Adult Basic Education*, Canada -- Department of Regional Economic Expansion (Ottawa: Queen's Printer, 1970).

Recommendations on Statistics of International Migration (N.Y.: United Nations, 1980).

General and Introductory Works

The Aging: Trends and Policies (New York: United Nations, 1975).

Cropley, A.J. (ed.). *Towards a System of Lifelong Education* (Toronto: Pergamon Press, 1980).

Cropley, A.J. (ed.). *Lifelong Education: A Stocktaking* (Hamburg: UNESCO Institution for Education, 1979).

Daoust, Gaetan (ed.). *L'éducation permanente et l'université québecoise* (Montréal: Les Presses de l'Université de Montréal, 1975).

Day, Gordon M. *The Abenaki Identity Project* (Canadian Ethnology Service -- National Museum of Man --Canadian Studies Report). Canada. The National Museums of Canada, No. 2e, 12/1977.

Draper, James A. and Alden, Harold. _The Continuing Education of Employees: A Review of Selected Policies in Ontario_ (Toronto: OISE, 1978).

Draves, Bill. _The Free University: A Model for Life-long Education_ (Chicago: Associan Press, 1980).

Hunter, Carman St. John and Harman, D. _Adult Illiteracy in the U.S.: A Report to the Ford Foundation_ (N.Y.: McGraw Hill, 1979).

Lengrand, Paul. _An Introduction to Lifelong Education_ (Switzerland: UNESCO, 1970).

Lovell, R. Bernard. _Adult Learning_ (London: Croom Helm, 1980).

MacDonald, Madeline. _The Education of Elités_ (The Open University Press, 1977).

Ross, David P. _The Canadian Fact Book on Income Distribution_ (Ottawa: The Canadian Council on Social Development, 1980).

Stone, Leroy O. and MacLean, Michael J. _Future Income Prospects for Canada's Senior Citizens_ (Montreal: Institute for Research on Public Policy, 1979).

Stone, Leroy O. and Marceau, Claude. _Canadian Population Trends and Public Policy Through the 1980s_ (Montreal: Institute for Research on Public Policy, 1977).

Swift, Donald and Skellington, Richard. _Inequality within Nations_ (The Open University Press, 1976).

Taylor, J. Garth. _A National Programme for Urgent Ethnology_ (Canadian Ethnology Service -- National Museum of Man -- Canadian Studies Report). Canada. The National Museums of Canada, No. 3e, 12/1977.

United Nations. _Recommendations on Statistics of International Migration_ (New York: Department of

International Economic and Social Affairs Statistical Office, 1980).

Weitz Harry. *The Foreign Experience with Income Maintenance for the Elderly* (Canada: Minister of Supply and Services, 1979).

Aging

Achenbaum, Andrew W. *Old Age in the New Land* (John Hopkins, 1978).

Binstock, R.H. and E. Shanas. *Handbook of Aging and the Social Sciences* (van Nostrand Reinhold, 1976).

Hobman, David. *The Impact of Aging* (Croom Helm, 1981).

Jarvik, L.F. *Aging Into the 21st Century* (Gardner Press, 1978).

Knox, Alan B. (ed.). *Programming for Adults Facing Mid-life Change* (San Francisco: Jossey Bass Inc., 1979).

Kuhlen, R.G. and Thompson, G.G. (eds.). *Psychological Studies of Human Development* (Appleton-Century Crofts, 1970).

Nicholson, John. *Seven Ages* (Fontana, 1980).

Phillipson, Chris. *The Emergence of Retirement* (University of Durham: Department of Sociology and Administration, 1979).

Preparation for Retirement: New Approaches (Beth Johnson Foundation, 1976).

United Nations. *The Aging: Trends and Policies* (New York: United Nations, Department of Economic and Social Affairs, 1975).

Van Tassel, D. *Aging, Death and the Completion of Being* (University of Pensylvania Press, 1979).

Aging: Canada

Allentuck, Andrew. *The Cost of Age* (Toronto: Fitzhenry & Whiteside, 1977).

Economic Council of Canada. *One in Three, Pensions for Canadians to 2030* (Hull: Minister of Supply and Services Canada, 1979).

Fales, Ann W.; MacKeracher, Dorothy and Vigoda, Deborah S. *Contexts of Aging in Canada* (Toronto: The Ontario Institute for Studies in Education, 1981).

Forcese, Dennis. *The Canadian Class Structure* (Toronto: McGraw--Hill, Ryerson Ltd., 1980).

Government of Canada. *Canadian Government Report on Aging* (Ottawa: Minister of Supply and Services, 1982).

Gutman, Gloria M. *Canada's Changing Age Structure: Implications for the Future* (Burnaby, B.C.: Simon Fraser University Publications, 1981).

Kettle, John. *The BIG Generation, Born 1951-66, Seven Million Canadians are Changing the Face of the Nation* (Toronto: McClelland and Stewart Limited, 1980).

Marshall, Victor W. *Aging in Canada (Social Perspectives)* (Don Mills, Ontario: Fitzhenry & Whiteside Ltd. 1980).

O.I.S.E. *The Elderly* (Association for Values Education and Research) (Toronto: The Ontario Institute for Studies in Education, 1978).

Retirement Without Tears, The Report of the Special Senate Committee on Retirement Age Policies (Ottawa: Minister of Supply and Services Canada, 1979).

Romaniuc, A. "Potentials for Population Growth in Canada: A Long Term Projection", in *A Population Policy for Canada* (Toronto: Conservation Council of Ontario and Family Planning Federation of Canada, 1974), pp. 4-19.

Statistics Canada. *Population Projections for Canada and the Provinces 1976-2001* (Ottawa: Statistics Canada, 1979).

Continuing Education

Apps, Jerry. *Study Skills: For Those Adults Returning to School* (New York: McGraw Hill, 1978).

Charters, Alexander N. et al. *Comparing Adult Education Worldwide* (San Francisco: Jossey Bass, 1981).

Cross, Kathryn Patricia. *Adults as Learners*, The Jossey-Bass series in higher education (San Francisco: Jossey-Bass Inc., 1981).

Cross, Wilbur. *You are Never Too Old to Learn* (N.Y.: McGraw-Hill, 1978).

Cunningham, Phyllis M. (ed.). *Yearbook of Adult and Continuing Education, 1980-81*, 6th edition (Chicago: Marquis Academic Media, 1980).

Daers, Larry Nolan. *Planning, Conducting and Evaluating Workshops: A Practitioner's Guide to Adult Education* (Austin, Texas: Learning Concepts, 1974).

Grabowski, Stanley M. *Paulo Freire: A Revolutionary Dilemma for the Adult Educator* (N.Y.: Syracuse University, Publications in C.E., 1972).

Hardgreaves, D. *Adult Literacy and Broadcasting: The BBC's experience*. A report to the Ford Foundation, 1980.

Harrington, Fred Harvey. *The Future of Adult Education* (San Francisco: Jossey-Bass, 1977).

Hesburgh, T.M. Miller, P.A. and Wharton, C.R. Patterns for Lifelong Learning (San Francisco: Jossey-Bass, 1973).

Ironside, Diana J. Innovations in Counselling of and Information-giving to Adult Learners in North America (Toronto: OISE, 1978).

Kassar-Bodson, Sophia and Thai, Quang-Nam. Télédocumentation la radio éducative actualisation" (Paris, France: Centre d'information et d'échanges-television, 1981).

Knowles, Malcolm Shepherd. The Modern Practice of Adult Education: From Pedagogy to Andragogy. Revised and updated (N.Y.: Association Press, 1980).

Kreitlow et al. (eds.). Examining Controversies in Adult Education (San Francisco: Jossey-Bass Inc., 1981).

Kulich, Jindra and Kruger, W. (eds.). The Universities and Adult Education in Europe (Vancouver: University of British Columbia, 1980).

Lawson, Kenneth H. Philosophical Concepts and Values in Adult Education (London: National Institute of Adult Education, 1975).

Little, Alan and Willey, Richard. Multi-ethnic Education: The Way Forward (London, England: Schools Council, 1981).

Lowe, John. The Education of Adults: A World Perspective (Paris: UNESCO Press, 1975).

Mayena, Serge. La Grande Aventure des Universités du Troisième Age (Brussels: I.E.I.A.S., 1981).

Mezizow, Jack D., Darkenwald, Gordon G. and Knox, Alan B. Last Gamble on Education: Dynamics of Adult Basic Education (Washington: Adult Education Association of the U.S.A., 1975).

Michael, J.A. (ed.). Adult Learning: Psychological Research and Applications (N.Y.: Wiley, 1977).

Newman, Michael. *The Poor Cousin: A Study of Adult Education* (London: George Allen & Unwin Ltd., 1979).

Organization for Economic Co-operation and Development. *Recurrent Education for the 1980's: Trends and Policies* (Paris: Centre for Education Research and Innovation, 1979).

Peters, John M. et al. *Building an Effective Adult Education Enterprise* (San Francisco: Jossey-Bass Inc., 1980).

Radcliffe, David. *Education and the Elderly in the United Kingdom*, a report prepared for the Adult Education Section of the Literacy, Adult Education and Rural Development Division of UNESCO (London, Ontario: Faculty of Education, The University of Western Ontario; and London, England: Department of Extra-mural Studies, University of London, 1980).

Solman, Lewis C. and Gordon, Joanne J. *The Characteristics and Needs of Adults in Post-Secondary Education* (Lexington, MA: D.C. Health and Education, 1981).

Stoikov, Vladimir. *The Economics of Recurrent Education and Training* (Geneva: ILO, 1975).

Teaching Adult Basic Education: A Program of Video Tapes and Written Materials for Teachers and Administrators (Toronto: OISE, 1977).

Thompson, Jane L. (ed.). *Adult Education for a Change* (London: Hutchinson, 1980).

Tough, Allen. *Expand Your Life (A Pocket Book for Personal Change)* (New York: College Entrance Examination Board, 1980).

Vanderheyden, Kees and Brunel, Louis. *University at Home* (Montreal: Harvest House, 1977).

Continuing Education -- Canada

Adam, R.J. et al. Education and Working Canadians. Report of the Commission of Inquiry on Educational Leave and Productivity, 1979.

Adult Learning, a Design for Action: A Comprehensive International Survey. International conference on Adult Education and Development (Toronto: Pergamon Press, 1978).

Armstrong, David P. Adult Learners of Low Educational Attainment: The Self-concepts, Backgrounds and Educative Behavior of Average and High Learning Adults of Low Educative Attainments (Toronto: OISE, 1971).

Aspects of Post-Secondary Education in Canada. Council of Ministers of Education, Canada, 1981.

Brouillet, Guy. Le temps du recyclage (Reflexions suscitées par la conference sur le recyclage des personnels d'enseignement (Toronto: Canadian Education Association/Association Canadienne d'éducation, 1980).

Brundage, Donald H. and Mackeracher, Dorothy. Adult Learning Principles and Their Application to Program Planning (Toronto: OISE, 1980).

Campbell, Duncan D. Adult Education as a Field of Study and Practice: Strategies for Development (Vancouver: Center for Continuing Education, University of British Columbia, 1977).

Continuing Education -- Saskatchewan. Annual Report 1978-79 [Regina] (Saskatchewan Department of Continuing Education, 1979).

Cook, Gail C.A. (ed.). Opportunity for Choice: A Goal for Women in Canada, Statistics Canada in association with the C.D. Howe Research Institute (Ottawa: Information Canada, 1976).

Council of Ministers of Education. *Aspects of Post-Secondary Education in Canada* (Canada: Secretariat of the Council of Ministers of Education, 1981).

Cropley, A.J. and Dave, R.H. *Lifelong Education and the Training of Teachers* (Toronto: Pergamon Press, 1978).

Cumming, Lawrence S. *Non-degree Continuing Education at the University of New Brunswick (Fredericton), 1978.*

Dickinson, Gary. *Teaching Adults: A Handbook for Instructors* (Toronto: New Press, 1973).

Fales, Ann W., MacKeracher, Dorothy and Vigoda, Deborah S. *Participant's Workbook* (Toronto: The Ontario Institute for Studies in Education, 1981).

Fleming, W.G. *Directions in Ontario Education* (Toronto: OISE, 1974).

Hall, Budd L. and Kidd, J. Roby (eds.). *Adult Learning: A Design for Action* (Toronto: Pergamon Press, 1978).

Hamilton, Marlene and Leo-Rhynie, Elsa. "Sex-role Stereotyping and Education: The Jamaican Perspective", *Interchange* 10:(2), 1979-80, 46-56.

Harvey, Ray Francis Ethelred. *Middle Range Education in Canada* (Toronto: Gage, 1973).

Humphreys, E. and Porter, J. *Part-time Studies and University Accessibility* (Ottawa, 1978).

Jones, Thomas Nelville. "Coming of Age", *College* 5(3) 10.

Keane, Patrick. *Adult Education and Community Development Studies in Canada* (Halifax, N.S.: Department of Education, Dalhousie University, 1980).

McLeod, T.H. (ed.). *Post-secondary Education in a Technological Society/L'enseignement post-secondaire dans une société technologique* (Montreal and London:

McGill-Queen's University Press, 1973).

Ostry, Sylvia. Canadian Higher Education in the Seventies (Ottawa: Information Canada, 1972).

Pipke, I. "Friend or Burglar: Program Planners Meet the Future", Canadian Journal of University Continuing Education, VII (2) 1981, 15-20.

Report of the Task Force on Post-secodary Education in Manitoba, 1973.

Review of National Policies for Education: Canada (Paris: Organization for Economic Co-operation and Development, 1976).

Roberts, H. "The ascription of adult education needs in Alberta and Quebec", Canadian Journal of University Continuing Education, VII (1), 8-11.

Skager, R. and Dave, R.H. Curriculum Evaluation for Lifelong Education (Toronto: Pergamon Press, 1977).

Skager, R. Lifelong Education and Evaluation Practice (Toronto: Pergamon Press, 1978).

Tough, Allen. "The Adult's Learning Projects". A Fresh Approach to Theory and Practice in Adult Learning (Toronto: The Ontario Institute for Studies in Education, 2nd edition, 1979).

Tough, Allen. Why Adults Learn. A Study of the Major Reasons for Beginning and Continuing a Learning Project (Toronto: The Ontario Institute for Studies in Education, 1968).

The Changing Educational Profile of Canadians, 1961-2000 (Ottawa: Statistics Canada, 1980).

"The Learning Revolution" in The Royal Bank of Canada -- Monthly Letter, Vol. 60, No. 4, April 1979.

"The Multi Levels of Continuing Education: Federal, State and Local Institutions", *Convergence* 12 (12), 1979, 40-50.

Continuing Education -- British Columbia

1979/80 Continuing Education Data (B.C.: Ministry of Education, British Columbia, 1980).

Continuing Education Activities, 1979-1980 (B.C.: University of British Columbia, 1980).

Directory of Special Projects: 1977-80. Ministry of Education, Continuing Education Division, April 1980.

Ironside, Anne and Buckland, Clare M. "The Women's Resources Center: A Coordinated Approach to Programs and Services for Women in Mid-life Change". In *Programming for Adults Facing Mid-life Change* (San Francisco: Jossey-Bass Inc., 1979), pp. 59-64.

Ministry of Education, B.C. A ministerial policy on the provision of: "Adult Basic Education Programs including English Language Training in the Public Education System of British Columbia" (Victoria, B.C.: Ministry of Education, Post-Secondary Department, Continuing Education Division, 8/1980).

Report of the Comittee on Adult Basic Education. Discussion paper (Ministry of Education, 1979).

Report of the Committee on Continuing and Community Education in British Columbia (Ministry of Education, December 1976).

The Mission of The University of British Columbia (B.C.: The University of British Columbia, 1979).

The Shifting Medical Paradigm: From Disease Prevention to Health Promotion: Proceedings (Vancouver, B.C.: The University of British Columbia, 1980).

Continuing Education -- Ontario

Attitudes of the Public Towards Schools in Ontario (Toronto: Canadian Gallup Poll Ltd., 1979).

Boards of Education and Adult Education: A Functional Definition of Continuing Education for Boards of Education in Ontario. Informal Publication (Toronto: OISE, 1979).

Cameron, D.M. *The Northern Dilemma: Public Policy and Post-Secondary Education in Northern Ontario* (Toronto: Ontario Economic Council, 1978).

Cassie, J.R.B. and Noble, Peter. "A Regional Perspective on Continuing Education; the Advantages of Getting Together", *Education Canada* 20(22), 1980, 35-39.

Central Statistical Services. *Social Indicators for Ontario 1977* (Ontario: Central Statistical Services, Ministry of Treasury, Economics and Intergovernmental Affairs, 1977).

Continuing Education: Ontario. A Review of Selected Policies in Ontario (Toronto: OISE, 1978).

Draper, James A. and Clark, Ralph J. *Adult Basic and Literacy Education: Teaching and support programs within selected colleges and universities in Canada* (Toronto: OISE, 1980).

Draper, James A. and Barer-Stein, Thelma. *Transition to Teaching Adults* (Toronto: OISE, 1979).

Hall, Oswald and Carlton, Richard. *Basic Skills at School and Work* (Toronto: Ontario Economic Council, 1977).

Hirschfeld, S. and Tracz, George S. *Telecommunications in Adult Education: A Look at the Possible Implications for the Coming Five and Ten Years* (Toronto: OISE, 1979).

Hudson, G. "Participatory Research by Indian Women in Northern Ontario Remote Communities", *Convergence*

13(1,2), 1980, 24-33.

Knoepfli, Heather E. and Saul, David J. *A Study of the Learning Needs and Interests of Ontario Adults* (The Ontario Educational Communications Authority, 1973).

Ministry of Education. *Continuing Education. The Third System* (Ministry of Colleges and Universities, February 1981).

Ontario Educational Communications Authority. *Strategy Papers for OECA: The Education of Adults* (Toronto: OECA, Research & Development Branch, 1973).

Report of the Commission on Post-Secondary Education in Ontario. *The Learning Society* (Toronto: Ontario Government Bookstore, 1972).

Skinner, J.M.R., Dilling, H.S. and McLoughlin, J.P. *Community Survey of Adult Education Needs* (Scarborough: Scarborough Board of Education, 1973).

Skelhorne, Jean M. *Adult Learner in the University: Does Anybody Care?* (Toronto: Department of Adult Education, OISE, 1975).

Vigoda, Debbie. *The Adult Learning Project*, 2nd edition (Thesis, OISE, 1978).

Waniewicz, Ignacy. *Demand for Part-Time Learning in Ontario* (Toronto: Ontario Educational Communications Authority, OISE, 1976).

Continuing Education -- Québec

Brunet, Roland. *Une école sans diplôme: Pour une éducation permanente* (Montréal: Hurtubise HMH, 1976).

Commission d'étude sur la formation des adultes. *Adult Education in Quebec: Possible Solutions* (Gouvernement du Québec, 1981).

La Sapinière Adult Education Conference. *The Adult Learner and the Future of Adult Education in Quebec,* Summary Report, May 14-15, 1980.

Report of the Royal Commission of Inquiry on *Education in the Province of Quebec,* Vol. II, 1964. Chapter IX, "Continuing Education", pp. 323-336.

Continuing Education -- Nova Scotia

Adult Education Program, Nova Scotia Department of Education. *Annual Report: August 1, 1978 - July 31, 1979.*

Jones, T.M. "Adult Education in Nova Scotia ... A Perspective", *Canadian Vocational Journal,* Vol. 16 (1980-81), pp. 4-6.

Immigrants

Employment and Immigration Canada. *Annual Report to Parliament on Immigration Levels,* 1980.

Jackson, J.W. and Pouskinsky, N. *Migration to Northern Mining Communities: Structural and Social-Psychological Dimensions* (Winnipeg: Centre for Settlement Studies, University of Manitoba, 1971).

Keller, Donald M. *Evaluation of Castle Zaremba: Effects on Language and Knowledge of Canadian Life* (Toronto: Ontario Educational Communications Authority, Research and Development Branch, 1972).

Richmond, Anthony H. and Warren E. Kalbach. *Factors in the Adjustment of Immigrants and Their Descendants.* 1971 Census Analytical Study prepared for Statistics Canada (Ottawa: Ministry of Supply and Services, 1980).

Labour

Denton, F.T., Robb, A.L. and Spencer, B.G. <u>Unemployment and Labour Force Behaviour of Young People: Evidence from Canada and Ontario</u>, published for Ontario Economic Council (Toronto: University of Toronto Press, 1980).

Denton, Frank T.; Feaver, Christine H. and Spencer, Byron G. <u>The Future Population and Labour Force of Canada: Projections to the Year 2051</u> (Canada: Minister of Supply and Services, 1980).

<u>Education and Working Canadians</u>, Report of the Commission of Inquiry on Educational Leave and Productivity (Canada: Minister of Supply and Services, 1979).

<u>Labour Market Development in 1980's</u> (Ottawa: Employment and Immigration Canada, 1981).

<u>The Development of an Employment Policy for Indian, Inuit and Metis People</u> (Ottawa: Employmentt and Immigration Canada, 1980).

Stolkov, Vladimir. <u>The Economics of Recurrent Education and Training</u> (Geneva: International Labour Office).

Literacy

Bataille, Leon (ed.). <u>A Turning Point for Literacy</u> (Paris: Pergamon Press, 1976).

Gilles, Lynette and Duggan, Kay. <u>The Adult Literacy Prime-time Learning System: A Preliminary Formative Evaluation</u> (Toronto: OISE, Research & Planning Division, 1979).

Jones, H.A. and Charnley, A.H. <u>Adult Literacy, a Study of Its Impact</u> (National Institute of Adult Education, 1975-77).

King, Kenneth J. "Research on Literacy and Work Among the

Rural Poor", Convergence, XII (3), 1979, pp. 32-41.

Murray, Alan. "The Literacy Debate: Sharing the Facts", Interchange, 7(4), 1976, pp. 19-23.

Thomas, Audrey M. Adult Basic Education and Literacy Activities in Canada 1975-76 (Toronto: World Literacy of Canada, 1976).

Values

Baba, V. and Janai, M. "Company Satisfaction, Company Commitment and Work Involvement", Industrial Relations, 31(13), 1976, pp. 434-447.

Bayles, Michael D. Morality and Population Policy (Alabama: The University of Alabama Press, 1980).

Bujold, Ch. "Signification du travail et valeurs de travail", in L'orientation professionnelle, 16(1), 1980, pp. 5-47.

Burstein, M., Tienhaara, N., Hewson, P. and Warrander, B. Canadian Work Values -- Findings of a Work Ethic Survey and a Job Satisfaction Survey (Ottawa: Department of Manpower and Immigration, 1975).

Campbell, A., Converse, P.E. and Rogers, W.L. The Quality of American Life (New York: Russel Sage, 1976).

Casserly, M.C. and Cote, L. The Work Importance Study in the Canadian Context (Ottawa: Employment and Immigration Canada, 1980).

Dumazedier, J. Sociology of Leisure (Amersdam: Elsevier, 1974).

Knasel, E.G., Super, D.E. and Kidd, J.M. Work Salience and Work Values: Their Dimensions, Assessment and Significance (Cambridge, England: National Institute for Careers Education and Counselling, 1981).

McCarrey, M.W., Edwards, S. and Jones, R. "The Influence of Ethnolinguistic Group Membership, Sex and Position Level on Motivational Orientation of Canadian Anglophone and Francophone Employees", *Canadian Journal of Behavioural Sciences*, 9(3), 1977, pp. 274-282.

Nightingale, D.V. "The French-Canadian Worker Shows up Well in the Study", *The Canadian Personnel and Industrial Relations Journal*, 22(5), 1975, pp. 28-30.

Peters, R.S. *Ethics and Education* (London: George Allen & Unwin Ltd., 1966).

Roberts, K. *Contemporary Society and the Growth of Leisure* (London: Longmans, 1978).

Roberts, K. *Leisure* (London: Longmans, 1970).

Strike, Kenneth A. and Egan, Kieran (eds.). *Ethics and Educational Policy* (London: Routledge and Kegan Paul Ltd., 1978).

Super, D.E. *Career Education and the Meaning of Work* (Washington: U.S. Government Printing Office, 1975).

Super, D.E. "A Life-Span, Life-Space Approach to Career Development", *Journal of Vocational Behaviour*, 16, 1980, pp. 282-298.